*f*P

Also by James L. Kugel

In the Valley of the Shadow

✦

On the Foundations of Religious Belief

*(and their connection
to a certain, fleeting state of mind)*

James L. Kugel

FREE PRESS

New York   London   Toronto   Sydney

FREE PRESS
A Division of Simon & Schuster, Inc.
1230 Avenue of the Americas
New York, NY 10020

First Free Press hardcover edition February 2011

FREE PRESS and colophon are trademarks of Simon & Schuster, Inc.

For information about special discounts for bulk purchases, please contact Simon & Schuster Special Sales at 1-866-506-1949 or business@simonandschuster.com.

The Simon & Schuster Speakers Bureau can bring authors to your live event. For more information or to book an event, contact the Simon & Schuster Speakers Bureau at 1-866-248-3049 or visit our website at www.simonspeakers.com.

DESIGNED BY ERICH HOBBING

Manufactured in the United States of America

1   3   5   7   9   10   8   6   4   2

Library of Congress Cataloging-in-Publication Data is available.

ISBN 978-1-4391-3009-4
ISBN 978-1-4391-5055-9 (ebook)

For R.

"Write!"—"For whom?"—"Write for the dead ones whom you loved in the past."—"Will they read me?"—"No."

Søren Kierkegaard, *Diary*

Contents

Dear Brooke, Elisabeth, Hanan, Michael, Yehuda,

Although I have spent most of my life as a professor, this book is not intended as a work of scholarship, but something that is at the same time more personal and more wide-ranging than the things that I usually write. Of course, some of what follows inevitably draws on my academic specialty, the Hebrew Bible, as well as on some wider readings in the related fields of religious studies and anthropology. In the end, however, what pushed me to write this was a desire to integrate what I have studied over a long period of time with what I have personally seen and felt. It hasn't always been easy, but throughout I have tried to be faithful to both . . .

In the Valley
of the Shadow

◆

I

The Background Music

In the summer of the year 2000, I began writing a book that would eventually be published as *The God of Old*. I had been working on it for about a week when I drove into Cambridge for my annual physical exam, and when I emerged an hour and a half later, I knew I had a pretty serious case of cancer. I was scheduled for a series of further tests the next week, so I didn't do anything (or tell anyone) right away; but eventually I had to break the news to my wife, and we went together to get the doctors' report on the tests.

The tests were not particularly encouraging. Today's doctors are—I suppose, largely as a result of malpractice lawsuits—extremely careful not to raise false hopes in their patients. They told us that the degree of degeneration in the cancerous cells taken in the biopsy was alarming, since it revealed a particularly aggressive form of the disease. I confess I don't remember much of the rest of what they said—something about cells "piercing the capsule" and making the prognosis even grimmer. "We probably can't cure the cancer," they said, "but we *can* treat it." They told us that, with proper care, I could expect to live at least another two years without debilitating symptoms, and that with all the new research and drugs becoming available, they hoped it would be possible to extend my life for two or three years more, perhaps even longer. I was 54 at the time.

The reason I am relating all this is because I want to recapture a certain state of mind that one enters under such circumstances. (I am sure many people who have gone through a similar experience will recognize what I am about to say.) After the initial shock, I was, of course, disturbed and worried. But the main change in my state of mind was that—I can't think of a better way to put it—the background music suddenly stopped. It had always been there, the music of daily life that's constantly going, the music of infinite time and possibilities; and now suddenly it was gone, replaced by *nothing,* just silence. There you are, one little person, sitting in the late-summer sun, with only a few things left to do. What should I do? Try to keep working on that book? You think: If I could make it through five more years, that would be generous. That would certainly be fair.

This was definitely a different perspective. But how could I have ever thought that life would just go on forever? I did, of course; that's what the music does, and everyone is caught up in it. The marvelous, often ironic writer William Saroyan is reported to have said on his deathbed: "I know everyone has to die, but somehow I always thought an exception would be made in my case." It's what we all think.

You learn all the shortcuts to the hospital and the best places to park in the underground garages. For some reason, hospital parking lots in Boston all seem to be staffed by recent immigrants from Eritrea and northern Ethiopia, refugees from a festering conflict. You get to know them, and after a while you even learn to say, "Hello—how are you this morning?" in their language (which is not Amharic, but either Tigrinya or Tigre). They smile in appreciation. You kid around with the nurses. But all this is just self-deception, trying to make this horrible, multiplex service center for the dying into something less ominous than it is.

Chemotherapy can be easy or not so easy—there are dozens of different regimes that go by that name, and in any case, different individuals respond differently to the same mix of drugs. It did not go very easily for me, and while this is not ultimately connected to the "music," it certainly had a role in what I thought and felt during those difficult days. I tried to get back to writing, but I just didn't have the strength. Life became very local: the bedroom, the bathroom, the kitchen. The people who love you loom large; their love is as tangible as bread. As for you, you are small. Your life is winding down now, and you can clearly see its end point; your life has become a compact, *little* thing. Good-bye. I have subsequently gone to many funerals, and I am always astonished by the smallness of the freshly dug, open holes you see here and there in the cemetery grounds. *Can a whole human being fit in there, a whole human life?* Yes. No problem.

> Do not rely on the mighty to save you, or on any human being.
> His breath gives out, then back to earth he goes—on that very
>   day, his projects are all for naught. (Psalm 146)

Days are planned around pills. Start off with a little codeine in the morning, then half a Percocet around lunchtime to get through the afternoon; follow up with the other half at night, plus extra-strength tylenol or ibuprofen as needed. (All this to counteract the effects of chemotherapy.) And then there are the chemo drugs themselves: the main ingredient in the blood thinner Coumadin is warfarin, which is also the main ingredient in mouse poison; not a comforting thought. (But what does it have to do with warfare? The Internet reveals all: *W*isconsin *A*lumni *R*esearch *F*oundation held the patent.) The mustine-based pills—those are the worst; the same chemical structure as the mustard gas used in World War I. Keep refrigerated. After a while, even coming close to the refrigerator makes you sick. Sometimes the chemo works too well, and I have to be admitted to the hospital for a couple of days. "Immune system?" the nurse says matter-of-factly. "You don't have an immune system." Then, pointing up at the IV dripping into my arm: "That's your immune system up there."

Back home, in the middle of the night, when things are almost pitch black, you pass by the dresser on your way to the bathroom and you imagine it all just being over, just done with. I don't want people to be sad. Later, staring up at the ceiling, you picture yourself being lifted up and crawling out of this painful skin, then walking around the room, free at last, a protoplasmic blob. That would feel nice. I didn't really think life would go on forever; actually, I was probably more obsessed with death than most people. But it was that music that threw me off, that kind of background buzz that keeps the illusion going.

O my God, do not take me halfway through life.
Your time stretches from age to age:
Long ago You created the earth, and even the sky is the work of
    Your hands; though they disappear, You will exist still.
All things tatter and fade like a garment; You cast them off like a
    change of clothes.
But You stay the same, and Your years never end. (Psalm 102)

In ancient Israel, God was deemed to be actually present in His temple, so someone with a desperate request might go there to be heard. These requests—some of them perhaps fashioned by the original supplicants, but others doubtless created in advance by temple officials for people to recite—are now found in the biblical book of Psalms. A few of them speak about death—though, interestingly, not that many: apparently ancient Israelites, like many other peoples, just accepted the inevitability of death as part of God's plan. What hurt, however, was dying before one's time: "O my God, do not take me halfway through life," as this psalm says. That was a violation of the pattern, so people must have wondered: how can such things happen? Perhaps, as the psalm suggests, it is precisely because God is eternal, "Your time stretches from age to age." From God's infinite point of view, people always die after an almost imperceptibly short period of time. They are small; ten or twenty years one way or another could hardly register with His eternity.

But the person who wrote this psalm was not, I think, offering it as a philosophical justification for his premature death. He was trying to get God to intervene:

> O Lord, hear my prayer, and let my cry come before You:
> Do not hide Your face from me in my time of trouble; hear me
>   when I cry out, and answer me soon.
> For my life is drifting away like smoke, as my bones burn in a
>   bonfire.
> My insides are dried up like grass, withered from lack of food.
> I've been groaning so much my ribs show through my skin.
>   (Psalm 102)

Reading these lines now, I don't have any trouble imagining the person who wrote them. He was very sick, perhaps in the last stages of some form of cancer. There was a good chance he would be dead in a few weeks or months . . . But he still had some hope. So he had dragged himself to the very place where God resides, the temple. If he could cry out there, he thought, perhaps God would hear him and intervene, since what was happening really wasn't normal, really didn't fit the pattern: "O my God, do not take me halfway through life."

You would think that a Bible professor would, in the circumstances I have described, seek comfort in these and other words from Scripture. But to be absolutely truthful, although I know much of the book of Psalms by heart, these were not the words that I kept thinking of after the doctors' diagnosis. Instead, what ran through my mind was mostly poetry in English, poems I had learned a long time ago—some of them fairly corny. Like Fairfax's song, memorized in rehearsals of our high school production of Gilbert and Sullivan's *The Yeomen of the Guard*. Poor Fairfax had been unjustly framed and sentenced to die. As he sat in his cell awaiting the executioner, he contemplated his fate:

> Is life a boon [a gift]?
> If so, it must befall

In the Valley of the Shadow

That Death, whene'er he call
Must call too soon.
Though fourscore years he give,
Yet one would pray to live
Another moon.
What kind of plaint have I,
Who perish in July?
Who perish in July?
I might have had to die,
Perchance, in June!
I might have had to die,
Perchance, in June!

In context, "July" means "in the middle of my natural lifetime"—
Fairfax is presumably in his thirties or forties. But better to have to
die now, Fairfax says, than to have had to die even earlier, in June.
(This reminds me of the old distinction between a pessimist and an
optimist. The pessimist says: "Things could never be worse than they
are now." The optimist says: "Oh yes they could!") But then Fairfax goes on to consider the opposite possibility—suppose life is not a
"boon" at all, but a curse from beginning to end:

Is life a thorn?
Then count it not a whit!
Nay count it not a whit,
Man is well done with it;
Soon as he's born
He should all means essay
To put the plague away;
And I, war-worn,
Poor captured fugitive,
My life most gladly give—
I might have had to live,
Another morn!

The Background Music

I might have had to live,
Another morn!

I like W. S. Gilbert's poetry (despite his occasional racism and anti-Semitism); I especially like his love affair with the letter "W" ("When a wooer goes a-wooing . . . ," "Willow, willow, waylee," "Oh weary wives, who widowhood would win . . . ," and so on). Deep thinker he was not, but he certainly had a good ear, and he was great at rhyming. Looking back on it now, though, I wonder why I could have found these lines so captivating. Life is neither a boon nor a thorn—it's just life, with its ups and downs, and most of us, for all the occasional downs, would prefer not to leave it, certainly not in June or July.

Another poet I kept thinking of was A. E. Housman, a man absolutely obsessed with death. In particular, I kept coming back to that famous poem of his that many students have to read in college English.

To an Athlete Dying Young

The time you won your town the race
We chaired you through the market-place;
Man and boy stood cheering by,
And home we brought you shoulder-high.

To-day, the road all runners come,
Shoulder-high we bring you home,
And set you at your threshold down,
Townsman of a stiller town.

Smart lad, to slip betimes away
From fields where glory does not stay,
And early though the laurel grows
It withers quicker than the rose.

Eyes the shady night has shut
Cannot see the record cut,
And silence sounds no worse than cheers
After earth has stopped the ears:

Now you will not swell the rout
Of lads that wore their honours out,
Runners whom renown outran
And the name died before the man.

So set, before its echoes fade,
The fleet foot on the sill of shade,
And hold to the low lintel up
The still-defended challenge-cup.

And round that early-laurelled head
Will flock to gaze the strengthless dead,
And find unwithered on its curls
The garland briefer than a girl's.

Housman was not only a poet; he was also a professor of classics at Cambridge University. In fact, he liked to describe poetry as a mere sideline; he saw himself primarily as a scholar of Latin and Greek literature. He also liked to say that his professional expertise had no influence on the poetry he himself wrote, but it is easy to see that this was not so. "To an Athlete . . ." is altogether imbued with the world of ancient Greece—the generic "athlete" as hero (a Greek notion through and through), the picture of Hades and its "strengthless dead," and the athlete's anonymous town, which might be located in Shropshire, but just as easily could have been found in the ancient hill country not far from Athens.

When you believe that your own death is not far off, however, none of this really matters. What spoke to me, I think, was this poem's view of dying too soon, or rather, its denial of the "too soon" part. There's nothing sudden or terrible about death here, it is just part of—more than that, the essence of—being a human being: first we carried you, "chaired you," through the idealized town square as our triumphant hero; now inevitably, symmetrically, we are carrying you along the same route to the grave. Too bad, you might say, that the time span separating these two events was shorter than it usually is: the athlete died before his time. But, on the other hand, perhaps it is really not too bad. After all, this is the "road all runners come," Housman says, and if you went down it a bit sooner than most, in the grand scheme, a few decades matter little (shades of Psalm 102). Meanwhile you did not have to live long enough to experience the vanity of human achievement firsthand, seeing the records that you broke broken anew by someone else, feeling your flesh slowly sag and fade, so that the athlete in you would disappear long before you did, and "the name died before the man."

The reader will perhaps have sensed that, looking back on these poems, I feel a little sheepish about them now—but perhaps that is precisely because those days seem so distant. The poems are more a curiosity than anything else, a souvenir from a bad time. In any case, they have no bearing on my subject, the background music stopping and the different sense of things that went with it. But there was another poem I kept thinking about during that period, one that is more directly connected to the state of mind I have been talking about. It doesn't say anything openly about death, but much more than any of the other poems I thought of, this one seemed to understand about the background music.

Rainer Maria Rilke (1875–1926) was the greatest poet of the German language in the last century, and one of his best-known poems is "The Merry-Go-Round," printed below. He wrote it while he was living in Paris, an expatriate. One day he wandered into a famous Parisian park, the Jardin du Luxembourg, and sat down on a bench. It is easy to picture the scene: The shy young poet, alone with his thoughts, looking up to observe some children riding on a nearby, rickety merry-go-round. The merry-go-round (which still exists) had its own little decorated roof, and beneath it, an assortment of various painted wooden animals—horses, lions, camels, an elephant—on which, as Rilke watched, the polite little French children took their seats. Nearby stood a brawny attendant, who operated a hand-pump that made the contraption turn around. As it gained momentum, it would go faster and faster until the time was up and the attendant would stop it. Here is Rilke's poem:

THE MERRY-GO-ROUND

Turning for a brief time in the shadow
of its roof is this revolving stand
of painted animals, all from the land
that lingers long before it fades away.

True, some are hitched to wagons; nonetheless
their faces make them still seem full of fight.
A fierce-looking red lion drifts along,
and now and then an elephant, all white.

Here comes a deer; it might be from the forest,
save that it has a saddle on its back,
to which a light-blue girl is safely strapped.

A boy in white leans on the lion's mane—
his little hand is clinging to the rein—
as the lion shows its fearsome teeth and bite.

And now and then an elephant, all white.

And on the horses sit some girls in bright
clothes, who seem somehow a little too grown up
for their horses' rhythmic prancing; in mid-jump
they gaze off, distracted by some distant sight . . .

And now and then an elephant, all white.

So on it goes, hurrying to the finish,
turning and circling for no goal or reason.
A red, a green, a gray go rushing by,
the shape of some child's outline, half-begun.
And time and again a smile is turned this way,
a happy one that dazzles, unrestrained
and squandered on this blind and breathless game.

Here, in the most literal sense, is someone for whom the music has stopped. He is positioned outside the merry-go-round's noisy world, a not-caught-up observer of those who are. And so he sits there. The poem's repeated line—"And now and then an elephant, all white"—is meant to duplicate for the reader the experience of watching from afar as that elephant keeps coming around again.

But time is what the poem is really interested in. Every child on the merry-go-round knows that the ride will be over soon; this is the whole sweet tension of being on a merry-go-round when you are a child. It lasts only "a brief time," according to the first stanza, and yet, when you are aware of the passing time, it actually seems to go on longer than you expected, though never long enough. By the same token, the animals are from the land that "lingers long before it fades away." (Rilke's *untergeht* really means "sinks" or "sets," like the sun dipping below the horizon.) This is of course childhood—those girls are already too big to be on this ride, thinking about other things—but it is also life itself, the way time works in life, going faster and faster. So, at the beginning of the poem, the colors are all connected to something, "a light-blue girl," "a red lion," "an elephant, all white," and so forth, but by the end, the merry-go-round whizzes so fast that all you see are the colors, "a red, a green, a gray," the half-begun outline of a child. And then the poem turns back to the observer and his summation of what he has been watching, caught in a disembodied flash: "a smile is turned this way, / a happy one that dazzles, / unrestrained and squandered on this blind and breathless game." Every poem has its secret nerves, and that simple, stupid word "happy" is one of them here: that is what we mostly are, *happy,* content in the midst of this awesome, one-time ride that we never really understand, this blind and breathless thing that has "no goal or reason" and ends too soon. Did Rilke know that he would die in his fifty-first year?

The fact that I am writing this now, seven years later, will indicate that the doctors were being overly cautious; as a matter of fact, they now say that I am cured, although (they always add) there is no iron-clad guarantee that the disease will not return. As for the music, I thought it would never start up again, but it has—gradually at first, with extended returns to the background-less, "real" state; but these returns eventually became shorter and more widely spaced, so that now the music is going almost all the time. Sometimes, however, if I concentrate hard, I can make it stop. Then everything about me that is all over the room, or all over the universe, gets sucked back inside, like one of those spring-loaded tape measures which, at the press of a button, pull the tape from wherever it has been spread out to back inside its little plastic case. When this happens and the background stops, I am suddenly just there again, down to the one, single person.

I have been studying religion most of my adult life, and if I try now to suggest that the background music suddenly stopping and the sense of smallness I have been describing have something to do with the whole world of religion, it is not without some hesitation. I know that public opinion polls consistently point out that 90 or 95 percent of all Americans believe in God; somehow, however, the good Lord must have arranged things for me to be miraculously sur-rounded by the unbelieving few, since most of the people with whom I have had occasion to speak on a regular basis (other professors, mostly, or else friends from the neighborhood) don't seem to be in this group of believers—at least they don't wear their belief on their sleeves. I suspect that many of them would be put off by a book about religion, especially one whose focus is something as fleeting and hard to pin down as the state of mind I have been describing. Nevertheless, that is the subject I wish to explore on the following pages. I perhaps should say at this point that one of my operating assumptions is that this state of mind reveals something essential about religion and the particular way of seeing the world that usually accompanies it. Or, to put it somewhat differently, I think that way of seeing the world involves a whole lot more than simply believing in God (or some other manifestation of the divine), or thinking about God, or somehow connecting things that happen in daily life to God's divine stewardship of the universe. As I hope will be clear, I don't wish to minimize this side of religion; but the way of seeing I am talking about has a great deal to do with how a person imagines himself or herself, imagines how that self fits into the world.

Long before the doctors' diagnosis, that background music had stopped for me every once in a while—as I'm sure it does for everyone, at least for a minute or two. Sometimes in the oddest places, for no reason at all: when you are just sitting on some park bench somewhere; or at a wedding, while everyone else is dancing and jumping around; or else one day standing in your backyard, as the sun streams down through the trees to land in a little dazzling square patch right in front of you. Then everything shimmers for a while and you are completely there, compact and contained. Rilke's picture of himself watching that merry-go-round evokes for me this same state. After all, the background music is all about living in infinite time, which is where we all usually live. But then it does sometimes happen that you are suddenly pulled inside yourself, like the tape measure I mentioned, and all that infinite time collapses.

No author, I think, has written about this particular view of things quite so poignantly as the author of the biblical book of Ecclesiastes, whose name in Hebrew was Koheleth. This writer was something of a renegade. Were it not for the fact that he was, apparently by mis-

take, identified as the great King Solomon,* his book would probably never have gained a place in sacred Scripture, since much of what
it says borders on the heretical. It differs from the rest of the Bible
not only in its general outlook, which has rightly been described as
skeptical and even cynical, but also, more specifically, in its particular sense of time. Elsewhere in the Bible, time is generally unidirectional, and what is significant about it are the historical events that
mark it off: first you were slaves in Egypt, then I freed you, and now
you live as your own masters in the land of Canaan. In Ecclesiastes,
time has a different quality. Things just keep repeating and cancel-
ing themselves out: for every action is an equal and opposite one that
moves things back to their starting point:

> "So futile," says Koheleth, "everything is so futile!"
> What does a person ever gain from all the effort he expends on
> this earth?
> One generation goes off and another comes in, but the earth stays
> the same forever.
> The sun rises and the sun sets; then, rushing back to its place, it
> rises again.
> The wind blows toward the south and then turns to the north,
> it turns and turns as it goes, the wind, and goes back again by its
> turning.
> All the rivers flow to the sea, but the sea is never full,
> [because] to the source of the rivers' flowing, there they flow back
> again . . .

---

* The opening verse identifies Koheleth as "a son of David, king in Jerusalem," and
he says later that he was "king over all of Israel in Jerusalem." By this he apparently
meant he was a descendant of David, hence, a member of the royal dynasty—perhaps
one of the governors appointed by the Persians to rule over "all of Israel" during the
period of Persian domination of the area (539–332 BCE). But a more literal turn of mind
apparently construed "son of David" as David's own son Solomon, who succeeded him
to the throne and did indeed rule over all of Israel in Jerusalem. The book's content
and, especially, its own Hebrew syntax and vocabulary identify it as belonging to the
Persian period and not David's.

What has been is what will be, and what was done will be done
again, for there is nothing new under the sun. (Ecclesiastes
1:2–9)

The words "everything is so futile" at the beginning of this passage serves as the book's oft-repeated refrain. It used to be translated
as "vanity of vanities," a beautifully resonant phrase, but one that
misrepresents somewhat the Hebrew word *hebel,* which does not
mean "vanity" in our sense, but rather anything fleeting and insub-
stantial, hence also, sometimes, ungraspable.

It seems that both senses of the word combine in the above passage.
It pains Koheleth to think that everything that happens, including
everything that we humans do, will eventually fade into insignificance—how futile, almost unfathomable! But this appears to him
the only possible conclusion. Eventually, even the most memorable
person is forgotten, and his or her great deeds are ultimately buried
in insignificance:

There is no remembrance of the earlier ones, and as for later
ones,
they too will have no remembrance with those who come after
them. (1:11)

We may know this truth in words, but somehow we never really
manage to internalize it, to really see ourselves for what we are. The
passage in this biblical book that most clearly expresses its author's
view of how we fit into the world is Ecclesiastes' famous "catalogue
of times." Americans of my generation tend to know this passage
because of its adaptation in a 1965 record by the Byrds (a then-
popular folk rock group). Unfortunately, that song—and the standard King James Version that it is based on—badly misconstrues
what Koheleth meant. The English says, "For every thing there is a
season, and a time to every purpose under heaven. A time to be born
and a time to die; a time to plant and a time to pluck up that which

is planted," and so forth. The implication seems to be that there is a time for everything in this life; you just have to wait, and the opportunity will come. But that's not at all what Koheleth meant.

> Everyone is in a season, [for] there is a time of [doing] each thing
>   in this world.
> A time of giving birth* and a time of dying.
> A time of planting and a time of uprooting what is planted.
> A time of killing and a time of healing.
> A time of breaking down and a time of building up.
> A time of weeping and a time of laughing.
> A time of mourning and a time of dancing.
> A time of throwing down stones and a time of gathering up
>   stones.
> A time of embracing and a time of shunning an embrace.
> A time of looking for and a time of losing.
> A time of keeping and a time of throwing away.
> A time of ripping and a time of sewing.
> A time of keeping silent and a time of speaking.
> A time of loving and a time of hating.
> A time of war and a time of peace.

> So what does a person gain from whatever he is working at? I considered all the activities that God has given people to occupy themselves with. He sets everyone right in his time, yet He also leaves something hidden in their minds, so that a person can never grasp what God has created from beginning to end. (3:1–11)

The last, long prose sentence is really the key to understanding the poetic catalogue that precedes it. For Koheleth, human life is a series of scenes that follow each other in succession. We have no con-

---

*Not "a time to be born"—that is a mistranslation—and not a time *to* do this or any of the other things in this catalogue. The Hebrew word translated as "to" is really an "of" here, that is, these times are assigned whether you want them or not.

trol over them—they just happen to us. And, as in the passage seen earlier, these things eventually cancel each other out: a person has children, but these births are canceled out by other deaths, hence, "a time of giving birth and a time of dying." Beyond this point, however, is another: although we may be aware of the changing seasons in a human life, says Koheleth, we never quite succeed in holding the whole thing together in our minds. There is always this "something hidden" that prevents us from really seeing ourselves for what we are. So we are constantly being caught up in all those wonderful or horrible things that humans see and do: the screeching baby, and the thud of dirt on a coffin; the rumble of mortar fire, and the way, on one glorious day, it stops; being with her, and then the grinding, grinding regret afterward, since those times are gone forever. Wherever we happen to be in life's various stages, we somehow lose sight of the whole thing, "so that a person can never grasp what God has created from beginning to end." This is our merry-go-round; we know full well that the time will soon be up, we even think about how time is passing, but—save for a privileged moment or two—the reality of it all somehow eludes us. We never quite see ourselves for what we are, utterly contained within our smallness.

2

Man Stands Powerless
Before Elevator

By the time I reached the middle of chemotherapy, I had many of the side effects that people suffer under such circumstances. But I could still keep doing some things as before. I kept on teaching, although only one day a week (for which I had to get fairly well doped up on painkillers). The only things I told my seminar students were not to come to class if they had a cold and to leave a few empty seats between them and me at the seminar table. People knew, of course; there was no hiding the light fuzz residue around my skull after most of my hair had fallen out. (Women have a slight advantage here: the hospital has women's wigs available for rent.)

When I passed my colleagues in the hall, I could see them wince. Usually, they wouldn't say anything. We had lost a senior colleague to cancer one year earlier, and now our longtime department secretary was in the last stages of breast cancer. What *could* they say? I kept thinking of another verse from the Psalms:

> My friends and companions stand back at the sight of my
> affliction; even those closest to me keep their distance.
> (Psalm 38:12)

I'm not sure what my colleagues were thinking. Outsiders often expect comedy writers to always see the funny side of everyday life and judges to be equally judicious in and out of court, and, I suppose, professors of religion to find some religious aspect to whatever they happen to encounter. But of course none of these is usually the case. Most people, when they see someone ravaged by chemotherapy, just tend—like the people in Psalm 38—to keep their distance, and I suppose that my colleagues, experts in ancient and medieval religion, were no exception. Fear also plays a role. "That could happen to me" is rarely spoken but often thought. (If people do talk to you about your condition, they usually get around to asking you what your first symptoms were—this could be useful information, after all! Some are also eager to discover something in your family history or some aberrant feature of your diet or daily regimen that can be blamed for your catastrophe while leaving them in the clear . . . All this, I am afraid, is merely human.) The sufferer, too, tends to leave his profession behind—the comedian, the judge, and even the medical doctor react, at least after a while, in no special way; they just sink into that passive state of patienthood shared by other sufferers. So I have no real explanation why, during this difficult time, I kept getting back to the matter of religion—I don't mean its practice, but the whole *idea* of religion and in particular, what it had to do with the state of mind described in the previous chapter, that feeling of the background music stopping and the sense of smallness, of discreteness, that accompanied it.

No one knows how or when religion began. For the last two hundred years or so, books on the subject have usually begun by noting that no utterly religion-less society has ever been observed—not in bygone days by European explorers pushing at the edges of Asia and Africa, nor, more recently, by ethnographers or other professional scholars tramping through the Amazon jungles or the rain forests of New Guinea. Indeed, the idea that all peoples worship *some* gods was used as a proof of the gods' existence way back in the time of classical Greece and Rome.

As a matter of fact, however, it is not entirely clear that any of this is true. There certainly are religions that do not involve actual gods or goddesses (some forms of Buddhism, for example), and perhaps a few societies even exist in which there is really nothing that corresponds to what might be called a religion of any sort. And beyond these observations is the rather obvious fact that, as humanity evolved, there must have been a time when our remotest ancestors were first learning to speak and in other ways to function as human beings. Certainly such creatures had nothing resembling a religion, indeed, the first humans could hardly be said to have *practiced* anything that might be described as worship or other religious rituals, or subscribed to anything like what we would call religious beliefs.

Still, the fact remains that, at a certain point, religions came into existence all over the globe and that, even today, they seem to be close to a universal feature of society. Almost everywhere on earth are temples, mosques, roadside shrines, sacred tents or lean-tos, holy rocks, holy mountains, storefront churches, mega-churches, cathedrals, monasteries, and ashrams, to which people repair with offerings of grain and oil and fruit piled high, of fresh-killed lambs and roosters still quivering from the knife, or else just ordinary pocket money, to be folded into the charity box or the plate when it is passed. All over the world people pray. "Our father, who art in heaven . . ." "O holy mother, who cares for all of her children . . ." "Spirit of our cattle camp, spirit of our fig-tree . . ." "Our father our king . . ." Stricken with cancer or some other dread disease, they seek not only the help of medicines, but help that comes from the other realm (though in some societies, the two are barely separate): what they ask for is, in the words of an old Jewish prayer, "the healing of the soul and the healing of the body" (two related but distinguishable items). And when they die, as all people eventually do, their survivors commit their physical and spiritual remains to the care of someone or something beyond the world of the senses; now they are on their "journey," and we can only wish them well.

All this has indeed been going on for a long time. One piece of evidence is the discovery by archaeologists of ancient burial sites in which, along with the bodies themselves, "grave goods" were also interred—primitive weapons or animal bones that presumably could be of use to the dead person in the next realm. Burial itself, of course, need have no connection to religious beliefs.* But taking your own, perfectly good weapon, or a quantity of red pigment, or even a usable animal jawbone, and giving it away to be buried alongside a lifeless corpse seems to bespeak some sort of belief that the dead person is, or sometime soon will be, alive in some other form or some other place. How far back this practice goes is still debated, but some scholars extend it well into Paleolithic times, 50,000 or even 100,000 years ago. In roughly the same time frame, scholars have found meticulous animal drawings and carvings in caves, as well as more abstract symbolic representations; these too may have served some purpose covered by the (admittedly multipurpose) label "religious." And long before humans could write anything down and so tell us their thoughts, people were combining their resources and bending their backs to build public temples and shrines, places of worship that soon grew to impressive proportions. What *were* these people thinking?

Part of my higher education was spent at the Graduate Center of the City University of New York, in midtown Manhattan. The Center's sleek white building was quite tall—it had, as I recall, something like twenty floors—and was served by a bank of elevators; you would go into the lobby, press the "up" button for the elevator, and wait. The elevator buttons were state-of-the-art for the 1970s: as soon as you

---

* Dead bodies quickly putrefy and so become a health hazard to the living. Burial clearly originated as one way of storing away the departed's body—rather than burning it or leaving it to be eaten by birds or wild beasts—while neutralizing the noxious hazards emanating from his corpse.

pressed the button, it would light up a bright orange color, indicating that your press had been registered and that the elevator was now on its way. Sometimes, however, it would take a while to arrive, and a crowd of people waiting would form in the lobby. I always found their behavior quite illogical and yet oddly familiar.

Someone who just arrived, seeing the orange button illuminated and five or six people already waiting, would often nevertheless approach the button and push it again. Nothing would happen, of course—the button was already lit. It did not even blink or flash; it just stayed the same. But somehow, pushing the button again just felt right to such people, as if they were in some way indicating that now one *more* person was waiting, so the elevator really should come down. Of course, most of the people using these elevators were graduate students and professors, and therefore probably not idiots; moreover, most of them had used this same bank of elevators day in and day out for at least a period of months, if not years, and knew perfectly well how the elevators worked. Surely these people understood on some rational level that pressing the same button more than once did absolutely no good. Nevertheless, they kept doing it. Indeed, *the same person* could often be observed pressing the button once, and then again after twenty or thirty seconds, and then again and again. I know, because that same person was sometimes me.

What is going on here? This behavior, inexplicable in rational terms, is nonetheless oddly familiar, and it might be summed up as "the need to do something." Man stands powerless before the elevator: it has no thoughts, and it has no way of registering *our* thoughts, our frustrations, or desperate pleadings. All it can do is what it has been designed to do, make all its intermediate stops before returning to the lobby. We know this, and yet we act as if we didn't. Why?

For modern naysayers, this is a model of the vanity of all religions: we all are powerless before the impersonal forces of nature, earthquakes and hurricanes and viruses and little cancer cells multiplying uncontrollably. But "the need to do something" nevertheless leads us into churches and temples, to light candles and say our prayers and seek out the aid of priests and shamans and other merchants of mumbo jumbo. "It couldn't hurt," says the Yiddish idiom; better to do something than do nothing at all. But at bottom it is all in vain, and at bottom, we ourselves know that this is so, no less than the button-pushing professors.

But to say this, and only this, is, I think, to miss what is essential in this picture. The need to do something—that part's certainly true. But going to church or saying prayers is really not the same as pressing the orange button, at least not for most people who pray. They don't "deep inside" know that it is a vain exercise; nor, on the other hand, do they do it because it necessarily works. As the French expression has it, *l'homme propose et Dieu dispose*—people can *suggest* (perhaps to others, perhaps to God in their prayers), but they can't do much more than that; God has the final disposition in the matter. So turning to God (or the gods) is a particular kind of "doing something." It's not doing nothing, but it is nonetheless a kind of submission, or—to take up my theme again—a kind of fitting into the world, of being no more than who one is. As a famous third-century rabbi put it: "Make His will your will, so that your will may be His."

Some civilizations seem to have this sort of outlook built in. For example, anyone who has lived for a time in the Arab world cannot fail to be impressed by what might be called the "explicit awareness of God" that permeates Arabic speech and culture. This certainly does not mean that Arabs are more moral or spiritual than anyone else—my experience, at least, is that people around the world are, after you get over the superficial differences, surprisingly, perhaps shockingly, similar. I simply mean that built in to the Arabic language and culture is a rather more explicit and frequent referring-to-God than is found in much of contemporary European or American life. The cliché that visitors to Arab lands return with is that everything there is punctuated by *"Insh'allah,"* a phrase that literally means, "If God wishes . . ." No speaker of Arabic can announce his or her plans for the future ("Next week I'm flying to Paris") or reasonable expectations ("After the baby's born . . .") without appending this phrase. True, it becomes rather automatic after a while, but it nevertheless seems to be an important piece of evidence of a somewhat different mentality: "People don't decide; God does." It would be arrogance, dangerously *punishable* arrogance, for you to act as if you alone determined your fate; God is big, and you are small. By the same token, if someone there asks how your mother's operation turned out, or just how things are going for you in general, the expected response is: "Everything's okay, *al-hamdulillah,*" the latter phrase meaning "praise to God," since He is obviously responsible for this state of affairs. If someone asks how many children you have, after you answer, the questioner must then say, "May God keep them safe for you."* The fellow who drove his cab with flawless daring or someone who just completed a great piano concert is told, "May He bless your hands." The standard chant in anti-American demonstrations (or the terrorist's shout as he blows himself up) is: *"Allah akbar!"* Grammarians are right to point out that this does not mean (as it is often translated) "God is great" so much as "God is the greater,"[1] that is, ultimately God's will is sure to triumph—by which is meant, of course: my cause, since it is axiomatically identified with God's will, has to win out in the long run. But why bring God into it when all you mean is, "Our struggle is just"?

No doubt an Arabic speaker† would be puzzled by this question. God is everywhere, and what He wants is obviously, incontro-

---

* This is of course a pious wish, but it is necessary in this specific case so as to invoke God's power against the Evil Eye, who might otherwise take advantage of having just heard a specific fact about you, a *number,* in order to harm you. (The same would be true, for example, of someone who asked your age.)

† I have been careful to say "Arab" and "Arabic speaker" rather than "Muslim," since I am really talking about a common cultural trait—it is as true, for example, of Arabic-speaking Christians as of Arabic-speaking Muslims. I don't doubt that some of this, being built into Islam, carries over to some extent to Muslims in other cultural environments; still, I would not describe it as a *product* of Islam, since, as I will say below, it seems to have preceded Islam historically.

vertibly, what will be done, even if things sometimes take a while to work themselves out. In the face of this all-powerful factor in every aspect of life, what do human beings or their little plans and desires count for? Earthly existence—*al-dunya* as it's called in Arabic—is just that, "down here"; what counts is what is decided "up there."

I don't wish to be misunderstood. In describing these things I am hardly maintaining that this view of life is without problems. The idea that God plans out everything that happens in the world is nice in theory, but in practice it raises the obvious questions: did He really plan the holocaust or AIDS or even the unjust death of a single infant? To this a modern believer can only say: such is God's will. More to the point, however, it is hard to believe that the idea of God's management of things did not raise similar questions in the ancient world, which certainly had its own share of large-scale brutality and murder, massive outbreaks of plague and famine, and a sickening, unceasing stream of infant deaths. Yet people back then still clung to God, indeed, loved God with all their heart and soul— why? A full answer, it seems to me, has to take account not only of God but of a certain way that humans had—and some still have—of conceiving of themselves and how they fit into the world. For them, their own being was existentially *small,* dwarfed by all that was outside of them.

The lesson was brought home to me some years ago when I heard an Iraqi Jew describe his first few years in the West after fleeing Baghdad in the 1950s. Back in Iraq, he said, there had been all sorts of Jews; some were "traditional," and others were, like his own family, "modern." (By *modern* I understood him to mean that they had basically given up traditional religious practice and lived a wholly secular life.) "But all of us, traditional or modern, knew one thing: God is very big, and man is very little. Once, some years after I had left Baghdad for the West, I went one evening to hear a famous theologian speak. I hoped that he would give me some piece of wisdom. But the more he spoke, the more his ideas and mine swirled around together in my head and the more upset I became. I could not get out of my mind this new thought: Man is very big, and God is very far away."

The religious smallness I have been talking about—the smallness of that summer and the months that followed—wasn't *in comparison* to anything, not to the great world outside or even to God. The book of Psalms says: "When I look up at the sky, the work of Your fingers, the moon and the stars that You have put in place—what is a man, that you should take notice of him, or a mere mortal, that you should take him into account?" Fine sentiments, but this is definitely not what I mean. What I have been trying to describe is not comparative, but absolute smallness—that (usually fleeting) sense one has of being no more than oneself, of fitting *physically* inside one's borders. The usual background—that background music I was talking about that surrounds us like a great, full-body halo, a mandorla into which we extend ourselves—disappears. Normally, I think, this is just a glimpse, something that comes and goes. But that particular summer after my diagnosis, it was never far from me.

I suppose one might naturally associate the features of everyday Arabic speech I mentioned with the religion of Islam (and even a Jew from Baghdad must have absorbed a good bit of the majority population's religion and ethos). After all, the word *islām* itself means "submission," that is, submission to God's will; a *muslim* is thus "one who submits."* Is not the pervasive deferring-to-God in Arabic simply a

---

* One often hears Muslims nowadays assert that their religion cannot have anything warlike about it, since the very word *islām* means "peace" in Arabic. But this is simply not so. It is true that Arabic *salām*, "peace," and *islām* do derive from a common Semitic root, Š-L-M, like *shelam* ("peace") and *ashlem* ("make one's peace with," "submit") in Aramaic. But a common root hardly makes for a common meaning, any more than it does for the words "radical" and "radish" in English. In fact it seems that the Arabic *islām* may ultimately derive from the Aramaic nuance of this root ("submit"), just as other Aramaic words were borrowed or calqued into Arabic via Islam.

reflection of a religion that preaches such deference? But someone familiar with the religions of the ancient Near East would probably find it more likely that the influence passed in the other direction, that is, that the peoples of that region had always deferred, and *ref*erred, to God or the gods in all things, going back to time immemorial, and that it was this mentality that helped to shape Islam as well as the various Arabic idioms mentioned above.

Names are one telling item. Throughout the ancient Near East it was customary to give children names that evoked one or another deity: "May-Shamash-guard-me," "Ishtar-is-queen-of-heaven," "Marduk-have-mercy-on-me," "May-El-protect-[this child]," and so forth. Some of these names have made it into English, thanks to the Bible. "John" was originally *Yohanan* ("The LORD has been gracious"), "Michael" is *mikha-el* ("Who is like God/El?"), Jonathan/*yonatan* ("The LORD has given"), and so on. The name "Hannibal" originally meant "Baal has been gracious," and the name of the Babylonian king Nebuchadnezzar (*Nabu-kudduru-nṣur*) meant, "O Nabu, guard my border-stone!" Gods are evoked in the proper names native to other societies as well, but the practice is certainly far less evidenced in today's European and American names, where Frank, Georges, Heinrich, Tatiana, and Tiffany hold sway.

The gods' looming presence in the ancient Near East had, of course, some practical consequences. People had to do the right thing—not just because the gods were watching, but because they were everything that man is not, powerful and permanent. Thus, one ancient Egyptian wisdom text warns readers against injustice,

> For man is clay and straw, and the god is his builder.
> He [the god] makes a thousand men poor as he wishes
> [Or] he makes a thousand men *as overseers,*
> When he [the man] is in his hour of life.
> (Instruction of Amen-em-opet)

A Mesopotamian text similarly warns:

My son, if you wish to be exalted, humble yourself before a god,
who can humble an [exalted] man [and exalt a lowly one].
What men's lips curse, a god will not curse . . .
The god will twist the twister's [i.e., liar's] mouth and tear out his
    tongue.

Aramaic Ahiqar (X 151–58)

Such sentiments of course have echoes in the Bible. When Hannah, mother of the prophet Samuel, praises God, it is in these terms:

Talk no more so very proudly, let no arrogance cross your lips!
For the LORD is a God who knows, and by Him are actions
    weighed.
The bows of the [once-]mighty are broken, while the weak are
    now girded with strength.
Those who were sated are hired out for bread, while those who
    were hungry grow fat with spoil.
The barren woman gives birth to seven, while the mother of
    many is bereft.
The LORD kills and brings back to life, sends down to Sheol and
    lifts up again.
The LORD makes poor and makes rich, He humbles and also
    exalts.

1 Samuel 2:3–7

Under such circumstances, it would simply be the height of foolishness to "talk so very proudly," to act as if God, or the gods, were not watching and that, as a consequence, one's life were entirely under one's own control. As the book of Proverbs observes, "Many are the projects in a person's mind, but the LORD's plan is the one that prevails" (Proverbs 19:21). Or again, "A man's mind may make arrangements, but God has the last word" (Proverbs 16:1).

✦ ✦ ✦

So it seems that how someone thinks about God—or if a person *can* even conceive of God in some real sense—has very much to do with how that person conceives of himself or herself, and more precisely, how such a self conceives of itself as fitting into the world. Implied in this observation is another, namely, that our present, Western way of fitting in—our big, clumsy, modern selves—is, in the grand scheme of things, somewhat unusual. A few centuries ago in the West, and even today in other large swaths of the globe (as reflected, inter alia, in Arabic expressions discussed above), a different sense of self seems to prevail.

The writings of many current ethnographers tell us as much: to this day in many parts of the world, the unit that really counts is still the family—indeed, the family in its most extended sense, the clan. In such societies you are, of course, *you,* but you are also, in both theory and practice, part of a larger unit that is making its collective way through life, having babies, burying its dead, watching on as one or another of its members prospers or fails—news of these things is *your* news and, soon, part of your life's story, since the things that happen to you personally are only part of who you are, one strand that rubs up against others (not always happily) in the great collective twine that is your real identity. What holds you and your clan together, of course, is your shared origins, that is, the parents and grandparents and so forth whom you all have in common, So-and-so's great aunt who was the sister of Such-and-such. And because this is so, they, though dead, are never far from mind.

The sociologist Peter Berger has highlighted the importance of this other "sense of self." In some societies, he notes,

there is no conception of the individual as sharply distinct from his collectivity. The individual's innermost being is considered to be the fact of his belonging to the collectivity – the clan, the tribe, the nation, or what not. The identification of the individual with all others with whom he significantly interacts makes for a merging of his being with theirs, both in happiness and in misfortune. The identification is typically apprehended as being congenital and thus inevitable for the individual. It is carried in his blood, and he cannot deny it unless he denies his own being.[2]

Some of the best ethnographic observations about sub-Saharan Africa in the 1960s were made not by a professional academic, but by a Polish journalist who lived and worked there, Ryszard Kapuszinski; his musings still have the ring of truth half a century later:

Individualism is highly prized in Europe, and perhaps nowhere more so than in America; in Africa, it is synonymous with unhappiness, with being accursed. African tradition is collectivist, for only in a harmonious group could one face the obstacles thrown up by nature. And one of the conditions of collective survival is the sharing of the smallest thing. One day a group of children surrounded me. I had a single piece of candy, which I placed in my open palm. The children stood motionless, staring. Finally, the oldest girl took the candy, bit it into pieces, and equitably distributed the bits . . .

If someone has become a government minister, replacing a white man, and has received his villa, garden, salary, and car, word of this quickly reaches the fortunate one's place of origin. It spreads like wildfire to neighboring villages. Joy and hope well up in the hearts of his most distant cousins. Soon they begin their pilgrimage to the capital. Once there, they easily locate their distinguished relative. They appear at the gate of his house, greet him, ritualistically sprinkle the ground with gin to thank the ancestors for such a felicitous turn of events, and then make themselves at home in the villa, in the yard, in the garden.[3]

Similar things have been written about other societies around the globe; here, for example, is the ethnographer Claude Lévi-Strauss:

For the Bororo [an Indian people from Brazil] . . . a man is not an individual but a . . . part of a sociological universe: the village

31

which has existed from the beginning of time, side by side with the physical universe, which is itself composed of animate beings—celestial bodies and meteorological phenomena.[4]

Likewise:

> In the Western view, the individual is a separate, autonomous entity that comprises distinct attributes (e.g., abilities, traits, motives, and values), and it is these attributes that are assumed to cause behavior. Further, there is a belief in the inherent separateness of distinct individuals. People seek to maintain *independence* from others and to discover and express their unique configuration of attributes. A great deal of what is known [to Western scientists] about "human" nature is rooted in this model of the person. Yet a growing volume of research by psychological and cultural anthropologists indicates that over three quarters of the world—the part of the world typically considered non-Western—does not share this view of the person. For example, many Eastern cultures neither assume nor value the overt separation and independence of individuals.[5]

In the broad perspective, our Western way of thinking of ourselves as individuals ("each in the cell of himself," wrote W. H. Auden), is rather new and unusual. Of course, that does not make us wrong and everyone else right; it is not a matter of right and wrong but of different perspectives and—this is crucial—the state of being and the way of perceiving that go with them. Obviously, being part of a clan—not just in theory, but to the extent that even a piece of candy has to be shared and that your relatives will troop in from afar and set up shop in your backyard without so much as a "by your leave"—imposes on each person a somewhat diminished sense of his or her own existence as an individual, and with it, a feeling that, yanked from the larger clan, he or she would not count for much; that is to say, in the shorthand I have been using, it imposes the beginnings of a sense of smallness. Everything about the world will look different from such a perspective.

> The spiritual world of the "African" (if one may use the term despite its gross simplification) is rich and complex, and his inner life is permeated by a profound religiosity. He believes in the coexistence of three different yet related worlds.
>
> The first is the one that surrounds us, the palpable and visible reality composed of living people, animals, and plants, as well as inanimate objects: stones, water, air. The second is the world of the ancestors, those who died before us, but who died, as it were, not completely, not finally, not absolutely. Indeed, in a metaphysical sense, they continue to exist, and are even capable of participating in our life, of influencing it, shaping it. That is why maintaining good relations with one's ancestors is a precondition of a successful life, and sometimes even of life itself. The third world is the rich kingdom of the spirits—spirits that exist independently, yet at the same time are present in every being, in every object, in everything and everywhere. At the head of these three worlds stands the Supreme Being, God. Many of the bus inscriptions speak of omnipresence and his unknown omnipotence: "God is everywhere," "God knows what he does," "God is mystery."

It is not difficult to imagine our own ancestors some generations ago living in such a world. Indeed, many of the things that Kapuszinski writes about Africans are easily paralleled by what we know of the ancient Near East, including the cult of the dead. Though largely forbidden by official, biblical law, consulting dead ancestors, contacting them through wizards or mediums—in fact, providing the deceased with water and sustenance on a regular basis via feeding tubes specially implanted at their burial sites (because, as Kapuszinski writes, these relatives have "died, as it were, not completely, not finally, not absolutely")—were practices that have been documented by archaeologists within biblical Israel and, more widely, all across the eastern Mediterranean, as well as in Mesopotamia and even in imperial Rome.[6] More generally, those three overlapping worlds Kapuszinski describes—one's physical surroundings, one's dead ancestors, and the whole world of God and the divine—have been described elsewhere by ethnographers working in such diverse locales as the Amazon rain forests, New Guinea, and Micronesia.

I should make it clear that in mentioning such things, I am not seeking to endorse their worldview, and certainly not to attribute any reality to necromancy and similar practices. The dead are dead, no doubt about it. Rather, my point is the "sense of self" revealed in the whole complex of these cultural manifestations. For centuries and millennia, we *were* small, dwarfed by gods and ancestors and a throbbing world of animate and inanimate beings all around us, each with its personal claim to existence no less valid than our own. So I don't think it would be wrong to say that "smallness" was, no less than the caveman's fat-poor diet and miles-long daily walking regime and everything else associated with his or her hunter-gatherer existence, simply part of humanity's natural state. We all used to be, axiomatically and for untold millennia, small. Is it too much of a stretch to suppose, therefore, that our brains, just as the other parts of our bodies, are still designed for this old way of seeing ourselves and fitting into the world, even though our current way of life and understanding of things have changed radically since then?

Thinking about these things that summer and fall, I also began to wonder if this sense of smallness didn't make it somehow easier to deal with all of life's ups and downs. Not for the reasons that might come to mind at first—that seeing oneself as merely part of some larger family or clan, or believing that one is being watched over by friendly, invisible forces, is a comfort in time of trouble. All this may be so, but that was not the essence of smallness as I saw it. Rather, the essence was something much more basic, a way of being that just seemed true: trimmed down, discrete, not taking anything for granted.

But I don't want to misstate the conclusion that might flow from these observations. I'm certainly not claiming that modern-day Arabs, sub-Saharan Africans, and noble savages everywhere walk about in the same sense of smallness that I have tried to describe. Rather, the things mentioned here—those little acts of referring to God in everyday Arabic speech, or in the names that ancient Semites used to give to their children, or the collective identity revealed in the solidarity of African clans—all these seemed to me that summer to be pointing to a very different way that human beings used to have of conceiving of themselves. Was believing in God (or the gods, or those ancestral spirits) itself a symptom, a clue about a particular cast of mind that was the sine qua non presupposed by all such beliefs in their essential form? Perhaps it all has to do with a certain sense—in privileged moments, a physical, bodily sense—of what one's own self really consists of, and where it leaves off. This, I remember thinking, was something I should really look into further—if ever I got the chance.

3

Hope

Another poem I liked to think about during the bad days was "Hope," by the American poet Randall Jarrell (1914–1965). I don't know when or why he wrote it, but it sounds like the work of someone who is trying to hold on, by his fingernails, to the slender chance that things may somehow change. In this poem, the possibility of hope takes the familiar form of the U.S. postal carrier. You never know what the next mail may bring:

HOPE

The letter killeth, but the spirit giveth life

The week is dealt out like a hand
That children pick up card by card.
One keeps getting the same hand.
One keeps getting the same card.

But twice a day—except on Saturday—
But every day—except on Sunday—
The wheel stops, there is a catch in Time:

In the Valley of the Shadow

With a hiss of soles, a rattle of tin,
My own gray Daemon pauses on the stair,
My own bald Fortune lifts me by the hair.

Woe's me! Woe's me! In Folly's mailbox
Still laughs the postcard, Hope;
Your uncle in Australia
Has died and you are Pope.
For many a soul has entertained
A Mailman unawares—
And as you cry, Impossible,
A step is on the stairs.

Of course, that's what it's like when you are close to hopeless: day after day the same hand, the same card, with the same big capital "C" in the upper right-hand corner. But then, you never know: sometimes, somehow, out of the blue, things do change. In the days when Jarrell wrote this poem, there were still two mail deliveries every day "except on Saturday," and of course none on Sunday. So, with those exceptions, hope was served up twice a day, like a hand of cards; letters would be dropped in the mail slot ("a rattle of tin") as the mailman ("My own gray Daemon [i.e., personal deity] . . . My own bald fortune") made his rounds.

What I like about the stanza in italics—which is actually a refrain stanza, since it is repeated in the second half of the poem (printed below)—is a minor point of technique. Poets can rhyme whatever they want, but rhyming two words in a poem inevitably yokes them together, suggesting that they have something in common. The effect of that suggestion can be almost anything—subtle, sublime, or just plain silly. In this stanza, Jarrell chose to link together "hope" and "pope"—which *is* just plain silly. After all, what *hope* do you or I have of ever getting a letter announcing that we have become *pope?* But in context this rhyme serves the poem's subtle, and actually sublime, message: "Look, anything can happen—you're not always in charge."*

Here is the second half:

> One keeps getting the same dream
> Delayed, marked *Postage Due,*
> The bill that one has paid
> Delayed, marked *Payment Due*—
>
> Twice a day, in a rotting mailbox,
> The white grubs are new:
> And Faith once more is mine
> Faithfully, but Charity
> Writes hopefully about a new
> Asylum—but Hope is as good as new.
>
> *Woe's me! Woe's me! In Folly's mailbox*
> *Still laughs the postcard, Hope;*
> *Your uncle in Australia*
> *Has died and you are Pope.*
> *For many a soul has entertained*
> *A Mailman unawares—*
> *And as you cry, Impossible,*
> *A step is on the stairs.*

The middle stanza may be a little confusing, but in it the mail has just now arrived, and it is, as usual, disappointing: Jarrell com-

* The mention of "Folly's mailbox" is actually an allusion to a line from Pope's "Essay on Man": "In folly's cup still laughs the bubble, joy." Less obvious is the biblical reference in this stanza. When Jarrell—who knew his Bible well—wrote "For many a soul has entertained a Mailman unawares," he was no doubt thinking of the reference to Abraham in the New Testament Letter to the Hebrews (King James version): "Be not forgetful to entertain strangers: for thereby some have entertained angels unawares."

pares the new, white envelopes that fill his "rotting mailbox" to disgusting "white grubs." He mentions three letters in particular, sent by the three traditional Christian virtues, Faith, Hope, and Charity (not coincidentally, each of these can sometimes be a woman's first name). But Faith's letter offers little other than her usual sign-off, "Yours faithfully"—thanks a lot!—while Charity's speaks *hopefully* of what? "A new asylum"—a word with chilling associations: a merely temporary refuge, or even a mental hospital. So the only letter that means anything is Hope's, because "Hope is as good as new," always. You never know when things might change: that mailman might really be an angel.

I actually had the occasion to meet Jarrell a year or so before he died. I was a college freshman, and I interviewed him for the student newspaper when he came to give a reading at our campus. He was a wonderful poet, with a wicked sense of humor. In one of his best poems, which I think he read that night, he describes a desperate, despairing woman doing her grocery shopping at the local supermarket:

> Moving from Cheer to Joy, from Joy to All,
> I take a box
> And add it to my wild rice, my Cornish game hens . . .

Here, the names of those popular laundry detergents are just the opposite of the speaker's own state of mind, which is beyond hope. That rare item is, alas, not readily boxed.

One Sunday, early on in my treatment, I was still in pretty good shape, so my wife and I decided to drive our kids to the mall—to give them the feeling that everything was still the way it had been. I remember that we ended up buying them an inordinate amount of stuff, mostly from the "Small Electronics" part of a large department store. The one thing I really needed was a raincoat, and in that same store I passed one that looked just right, dark blue, on sale. I tried it on. "But what's the point?" I remember thinking. "Why spend money on something I may wear six or seven times?" I remember we even walked out of the store without buying it, but in the parking lot, I decided—I'm not sure why—to go back and get it anyway. I still have it.

After Jarrell died, some of the poems he had never published during his lifetime were included in his posthumous *Complete Poems*.[1] This one may be among the very last things he wrote in 1965:

WHAT'S THE RIDDLE . . .

"What's the riddle that they ask you
When you're young and you say, 'I don't know,'
But that later on you will know—
The riddle that they ask you
When you're old and you say, 'I don't know,'
And that's the answer?"

"I don't know."

4

Religion on the Brain

That feeling of the music stopped, and the sense of smallness—of being able to fit inside one's borders, without drifting off into the great world all around—these are hard to recapture nowadays. But then they were everything; they kept following me around, and I felt it was somehow important to try to look into all this at some point. I knew that researchers were busy investigating the whole phenomenon of religion from various new angles, and it seemed to me that the sense of things that I have described should certainly be part of the overall picture.

Before hard science entered the fray (about thirty years ago), scholars and ordinary laymen had a battery of explanations for the widespread existence of religion. Religion, it used to be said, arose in primitive man in order to answer questions about the world that otherwise would go unanswered; or else it sprang up in order to allay people's fears of the unknown, especially the fear of death; or else it simply reflected an innate human love of the irrational (the same force that leads people today to believe in UFOs and extra-sensory perception). Particularly common were explanations for the existence of religion in terms of the social good it provided: its purpose was to ensure that people behave properly and cooperate with each other. To that end, societies developed a set of beliefs about the gods and the rules they gave us to live by—strictly enforced by those same gods. As for sacrifices, dances, and other religious rituals, these existed in order to impress common people with the gods' power, as well as to further inculcate the gods' rules.[1]

What all these explanations share is the fundamental notion that *people* invented religion—indeed, kept inventing it over and over again in different societies—because it served one or more useful purposes. This approach was generally predicated on, sometimes quite explicitly, a fundamental atheism: there really is no God, nothing in reality that might answer to the name "divine." Instead, divinity is a human creation designed for some human good—for example, to keep primitive savages from robbing, raping, and killing at will.[2] Over the last two decades, however, most of these explanations have been abandoned—not because the scientists have suddenly "got religion," but because the actual fieldwork of anthropologists and, still more important, the groundbreaking work of lab scientists, have suggested a host of new, more scientifically grounded, explanations.[3]

Thus, evolutionary biologists have sought to connect the near-universal character of religion with the way the human brain evolved through various stages of its development. If almost all human societies exhibit things that we would describe as belonging to the "religious" category—such as a belief in supernatural beings and/or in an "unseen realm"; the efficacy of sacrifice, prayer, and similar acts, and the various community rituals connected with any of these; the need for priests, shamans, and other spiritual intermediaries; laws, teachings, and secret lore all associated with the realm of the divine; and so forth—these things must have emerged in part because of the way evolutionary pressures have shaped our brains and, in consequence, our behavior.

Over the past few years, some of these theories have been popularized and have become the subject of much public debate. I must confess that the conduct of this debate has often struck me as a bit silly. The version of religion presented by its detractors seems rather narrow and strikingly simpleminded, while religion's defenders have set for themselves the enviable task of telling their readers precisely what they want to hear, which is, for the most part, liberal Protestant theology. But the research was still pretty new in the year of my diagnosis, and far less polemical. I actually found much of it suggestive with regard to the particular state of mind I kept thinking about.

Part of this research began with the observation that all kinds of species on earth have developed different ways of detecting potential predators. Their bodies evolved organ systems that allow them to smell, see, hear, or in some other way discover an approaching enemy. These detection systems are, quite literally, lifesavers, and so in many species they work to excess, often producing a false positive. Your dog jumps up at the sound of *anyone* passing in the street, friend or foe, or sometimes even at the noise made when snow slides off your roof in midwinter and falls in a clump next to your house. Jumping up and barking of course costs the dog something in wasted energy, but it is definitely worth it: one time out of a hundred or a thousand, what he hears or smells may indeed be some kind of threat. Scholars have described this phenomenon as a *hair-trigger agency detector* or a *hyperactive agent detection device* in the brains of dogs and all sorts of other animals: the animal detects an *agent*—someone or something capable of inflicting harm (as opposed to other smells, sounds, or sights that are altogether unthreatening)—but the part of the brain that does the detecting is *hyperactive,* working overtime and producing a certain number of false positives.[4] This feature is found in the brains of a wide variety of species.

When it comes to higher species, scholars have shown that brains can be particularly sophisticated: they can choose between different reactions to a potential predator (that is, to flee or fight) on the basis of their assessment of the overall situation and the specific predator's aims. With human beings, figuring out what an advancing predator intends reached new heights, especially since one sort of threat our ancestors faced emanated from other human beings. *What is that guy coming toward me thinking? Should I run away, stay and fight, or throw my arms around him like a long-lost brother? And what does* he *think* I *might do?* This involves making a rather complicated set of judgments—first realizing that the advancing threat is a *thinking* agent, and then trying to think what he thinks, and even trying to think what he thinks I think. In this exercise, repeated ad infinitum in daily life, the human ability to attribute cognition to others plays a crucial role. But ultimately, at least according to some scholars, it caused early humans to overreact and attribute humanlike cognition to things that in fact have no capacity for thought. Then the river, the rain clouds, and the sun in the sky, because they appear to be agents on which our existence depends, take on a new look. They, or the little someone inside them that makes them go, must be deciding at this very moment what to do next, how to treat us next. In this some evolutionary biologists find the seeds of one aspect of religion, the attribution of cognition to phenomena from the natural world, or rather, to the gods and goddesses deemed to control them.[5]

In this approach to understanding the origins of religion, the architect's notion of a *spandrel* is sometimes invoked.[6] A spandrel is a by-product of something that an architect creates. For example, the architect wants a set of stairs joining the main floor to the one above it, since it will be far easier for the house's inhabitants to walk up a set of stairs than, say, to climb up a rope ladder. But in creating such a staircase, the architect willy-nilly creates a "dead space" underneath the stairs. True, that space may eventually be put to some use—a set of shelves can be installed there, or a broom closet can take up at least part of the area—but these are altogether secondary to the architect's original purpose in creating the staircase. Once in place, however, the dead space can take on a life of its own. It may, for example, become the lighted showcase for the householder's collection of ancient Roman glass—such an important part of the house that one loses sight of the fact that this center of attention was originally a spandrel.

Biologists know about biological spandrels from their study of evolution. A particular physical feature evolves for one purpose, but in so doing some other feature emerges as a by-product, or the same feature comes to fulfill an entirely different purpose (a process now known as "exaptation").[7] The feathers on a bird's body, for example, appear to have first evolved in order to help regulate body temperature. It was only later in these creatures' evolution that these appurtenances came to serve an entirely different purpose: flight. And since evolution proceeds in linear fashion, there are also all kinds of useless aspects of living forms that survive despite their uselessness, such as the "vestigial organs" pointed out by Darwin and others. Thus, the wings of an emu or the vestigial toes of horses serve no useful purpose; they are leftovers from an earlier stage in the creature's emergence. So too, the analogy goes, with religion: human beings' willingness to attribute this or that effect to some unseen deity may simply be a spandrel created along with some useful feature of the evolving human brain—the hair-trigger agency detector that has otherwise proven so useful in our dealings with potential predators.

Some of this struck me at the time as mere theorizing (and indeed, somewhat problematic theorizing at that). But I knew that at least the underlying idea that our brains have been shaped by our evolution as a species—so that we are now, in a sense, born preprogrammed to think in certain ways and not others, to *perceive* in certain ways and not others—has been demonstrated repeatedly through ingenious experiments with human and animal subjects, as well as through clinical observations by neurologists treating brain injuries. These data seemed to give the lie to what used to be the common wisdom, that infant brains are all essentially a *tabula rasa* on which, day by day, new lessons are inscribed, until the child learns how to walk and talk and do all the other things that humans do. Not at all, it seems. Rather, we are all born with brains that have been designed to perceive in very specific ways and perform certain tasks.[8]

The case has been proven most dramatically with regard to language. (I actually had studied some of this even before I got sick.) Infants are not born with a linguistic "blank slate" at all. Rather, their brains come prefitted with an area for absorbing linguistic information—not just absorbing it, but actually sorting the bits of speech they first hear into preestablished categories. That's how they learn to speak in what would otherwise appear to be an impossibly short period of time: they have been programmed in advance to help them make sense of those odd noises emanating from the big faces leaning over their cribs. It follows that *all* the various languages that humans speak all over the globe share certain structural features—these languages all necessarily conform to the same pre-established patterns hardwired into our brains. Linguists have shown this to be true in various ways. Analysis of syntax—the patterns by which words are combined with each other into sentences—in unrelated languages has shown that, despite all the superficial differences, these languages all have nouns and verbs that interact in similar ways, and, equally important, that none of them demonstrates certain sorts of interactions which, although logically possible, just do not seem to be part of the human repertoire. For example, a statement in English can often be turned into a question by putting the verb at the head:

> The hunters are in the field.
> Are the hunters in the field?

But suppose the sentence is a bit more complicated:

> The hunters who are chasing the fox are in the field.

Here the word *are* appears twice. But we don't latch onto the first *are* and stick it at the head of the sentence to make the question:

> Are the hunters who chasing the fox are in the field?

The reason is that our brain doesn't process sentences as simple sequences of words ("first word," "second word," "third word," and so on) but rather automatically sorts them into grammatical catego-

48

ries, "subject phrase," "main verb," and so forth. That's what allows us to recognize the first *are* as part of the sentence's complex subject, "the hunters who are chasing the fox," and therefore to hold out for the second *are* for the inversion:

Are the hunters who are chasing the fox in the field?

But why shouldn't we just seize on the first verb we come across and form a question by sticking it at the head of the sentence? By the same token, a human language might theoretically form questions by taking the very last item in the declarative sentence and sticking it at the head of a question, no matter what its grammatical function—for example:

Field are the hunters who are chasing the fox in the?

But we don't do that either, because our minds are set up to process not random sequences of words, but grammatical categories.[9]

Doctors studying certain types of brain injuries have offered further evidence that we are preprogrammed for language: specific parts of the brain appear to be allocated not to speech in general, but to some rather specific subcategory of speech. Thus, some patients who have suffered one particular sort of damage to the brain (an injury to that part of the brain known as Wernicke's area) have been found to be capable of speech of a sort, but they experience difficulty in producing nouns when they speak. Indeed, sometimes the language deficit is even more specific: some aphasia patients have been found capable of producing names of objects like "table" and "chair," but not abstract nouns like "independence" or "love." Other patients have precisely the opposite problem. "One patient could not name fruits or vegetables: he could name an abacus and a sphinx, but not an apple or a peach."[10] All this suggests that, when it comes to speech, the human brain does not start off as a blank slate at all: rather, it looks more like an assemblage of linguistic boxes, preestablished places into which are sorted all the particulars of the language to which an infant is first exposed.

If this is true of speech, it seems highly likely that it is true of other things as well: our brains are predisposed to perceive certain things (and perhaps *not* to perceive others), to have us act in certain ways but, generally speaking, not to act in others. To mention only some of the most obvious candidates: all human beings smile, laugh, and cry. In fact, recent studies have shown that the facial expressions by which we show our emotions—fear, happiness, anger, sadness, surprise, and so forth—are pretty much the same all over the world.[11] But there is no logical reason why they should be. Why couldn't scrunching up your eyebrows and glaring be a sign of anger in one society and a sign of deep affection in another? That would certainly be possible if facial expressions were merely a societal convention. So the fact that our faces all do the same thing when we're angry or when we're sad is a strong indication that these bits of behavior are hardwired into our brains at birth.

And how far does the programming go? One interesting area of research has to do with our perception of colors. Since the different colors that our eyes see are really only segments on one great, continuous spectrum of color, there is nothing *natural* about where our languages decide that one color leaves off and another begins. Theoretically, what we call red and orange could be identified as one and the same color in some other language. By the same token, all the different shades that English calls "blue" (true, we sometimes further specify that this is cobalt blue while that is turquoise blue—still, both are indisputably *blue* in English) might be identified in another language as two completely different colors, *zapalop* and *konderak*. And indeed, this turns out to be the case. In fact, early anthropologists were surprised to discover that many languages have nothing corresponding to the array of color words in English or other Western languages. Some languages seemed to recognize only two colors, "black" and "white."

This led researchers to what appeared to be a logical conclusion.

People who lived in one society or another would not have been con-
ditioned to *see* color distinctions if their language didn't have words
for them. For example, if you spoke a language that had only four
color words—say, white, black, red, and green—then anything blue
or purple or brown would just be assimilated in your perception to
the nearest color you did have a word for. As a result, your eyes just
wouldn't notice that one thing was blue and another was green; they
would both be perceived as the same color.

Field studies have shown that this is nonsense—people distinguish
colors just fine, no matter what their languages have or do not have
words for. But researchers have also come across a most surprising
fact. Studying an array of color terms in some ninety-eight different
languages across the globe, they found that no language studied had
more than eleven basic color terms—and that they always focused
around the same colors: white, black, red, green, yellow, blue, brown,
purple, pink, orange, and gray.[12] (Not all languages had words for all
eleven, of course, and "basic" did not include compound expressions
like "bluish-purple" or "pumpkin-colored.") Once the researchers
had established the color terms in a given language, they then asked
native speakers of the language to show on a color chart where one
color left off and the next began (the chart contained some 329 different color chips), as well as to identify the chip that best typified
each color term in their language. There were clear differences in
a color term's "spread"—obviously, the fewer terms there were in a
language, the more chips each term would cover. Yet interestingly,
the focal point of each basic color was the same from language to
language. For example, in a theoretical language in which there
were only three color terms—say, *gzand* (which included our black),
phthox (which included our white), and *sprong* (which included our
red)—then, although *sprong* also included some pinks, oranges, purples, browns, and so forth, the informants would always point to
what we would call a "red" chip as the focal center of *sprong,* while
the oranges, purples, and browns would be satellite shades clustered
around the red center. Logically, of course, there is no reason why

this should be so. And yet it is so. This suggests that *red* is just some-how hardwired into our brain as a basic color—whether we have a word for it or not, and no matter how many other color terms there are in our language.[13]

But there's more. Scholars discovered that even the *order* in which color distinctions come is quite fixed. That is, if a language recog-nizes only two colors, they will always focus on what we call black and white (or "dark" and "light")—not black and red or green and purple; black and white. When a third term appears, it will invari-ably correspond to our red, and when there is a fourth term, it will be either green or yellow; and so on. All this seems to have been imprinted in our brains before birth.

Using such data as their starting point, some ethnographers have sought to establish a complete list of "universals" in human thought and behavior—not just color distinctions, but all sorts of other things that seem to be found in all societies around the globe.[14] Some of them are pretty obvious: not surprisingly, all societies have "cook-ing," "kinship classifications," "laws and rules," and "units of time." But others are a bit more intriguing: Why should all societies exhibit such features as music and dancing, the concept of some collective identity, "coyness display" among young women, a concept of fair-ness and "distinguishing right from wrong"—as well, of course, as "belief in the supernatural/religion"? Do people everywhere share these things because they are endlessly reinvented, a natural out-growth of the human condition? Or is there something inside our heads that predisposes us to make music (and poetry) and to have categories like right and wrong? The question might even be mod-ified slightly. Perhaps indeed these predispositions were not there from the beginning—we certainly did not inherit them from our primate ancestors. But the human brain, like the rest of the human body, gradually evolved. Thus (to return to an earlier example) the role of speech became increasingly important, and as this occurred, our brains came to be more and more configured, and specialized, so as to meet this need. Similarly, as humans developed, so did cer-

tain other kinds of interactions—and soon these too began to leave their mark on our brains, predisposing them to function in certain ways. The question about religion that all of this has raised is: are our brains somehow programmed in such a way as to lead people all over the world to develop religions?

When it comes to the state of mind that is my subject here—that is, the sharply different way I saw things (and saw myself) that summer of my diagnosis—all this research seemed highly suggestive. The idea that human brains are specially outfitted, *predetermined* to function along certain lines (and therefore, perhaps, tipped to perceive certain things and not others) seemed to go well with everything I have been trying to describe.

But other parts of the modern theorizing about religion appeared a lot less convincing to me—in particular the assumption mentioned earlier that the starting point of religion is the attribution of agency (to a god or gods, to sun and moon, to this tree and that stream). To say this is to walk right by the very state of mind that I have described. It is the sense of smallness and discreteness, of fitting into a much larger world (and a world that is not passive, but looms and overshadows)—it is this sense of things that was the patrimony of human beings since human beings began, long before there was anything like a religion. In fact, it seemed to me, it was this sense of things that made religious perception possible in the first place. Into this baseline sort of religious consciousness first came an awareness not of "gods," but of God Undifferentiated, indistinguishable from everything that was part of the great, looming Outside. This was what people saw, smelled, and heard—as real as anything we see today. Along with this awareness came a fundamental openness to the Outside, and the particular way of fitting into the world that this openness implied; the gods come later.[15] These things may be hard to talk about, but they really can't be ignored (as they have been). In fact, the "early man" of a lot of these recent studies is, if you look closely at him, a rather odd amalgam. He wears a primitive loincloth, but if your eyes travel upward they will eventually come to the well-trimmed beard and black-rimmed reading glasses of an MIT professor, that is to say, to a thoroughly modern self. The theorist's real task is not to project his own kind of self back onto primitive man, but to try to discover a different sort of self and its own, very different way of perceiving, indeed, to discover the whole vast world that it perceived.

5

Under Sentence of Death

If you have been diagnosed with a dangerous cancer, you don't stop being the person you were before the diagnosis—in fact, you end up doing a lot of the same things you used to do—but you are not even remotely the same. It is not only that you have this new, time-consuming occupation, *being treated.* There is also—always—that enormous thing suspended above and not far in front of you wherever you go, and it changes everything about how you think about yourself.

At first, it's as if there's just something wrong, some *little* thing that you can't seem to shake. So you can never quite let yourself get completely caught up at a kid's birthday party, or a lecture that you're giving, or whatever you're working on. Right in the middle, you remember—or, really, it remembers you. It's a bit like those post-Renaissance paintings of a beautiful garden or a rustic valley in which fleshly maidens and handsome swains are engaged in a feast, while tucked off in the background, in some corner, so that you hardly notice him at first, is the figure of Death and the inscription "Et in Arcadia ego" ("even in Arcadia"—the idealized pastoral region of ancient Greece—"am I"). That little reminder never leaves you—or else it does leave you for a little while, but then it comes back. Still, you do have some hope; lots of people survive. Later on, though . . . well, you just learn to concentrate harder.

Last week I saw a friend of mine concentrating in that way. We were at a meeting; he's also a professor, but younger—early 50s, I'd say. "Professor" conjures up the wrong image: actually, he's well over six feet and very powerful about the arms and shoulders—for most people, getting into a physical fight with him would be a joke. But he's known for almost six months that the cancer has spread to his liver; there's not much more that chemo can do. He still looks tough, but much thinner, and at the meeting his remaining hair was matted down onto his head in wet-looking clumps. He used to be very upbeat about what was happening; now he's just completely focused on the next thing, on the next agenda item at the meeting. He hasn't lost his sense of humor, but his laugh tends to trail off more quickly than it once did. When he asked me what I was working on these days, I hesitated for a while, but I finally said I was trying to write something about "the illness." He smiled. "Oh yes," he said. "Those books are always written by the people who got better."

Anicius Manlius Severinus Boethius (ca. 480–ca. 525 C.E.) was an early Christian philosopher, born to one of the leading noble families in Rome. His privileged position in society afforded him a thorough education in Greek and Roman learning, and he spent much of his short life at leisure, translating and commenting on Greek philosophical treatises as well as composing works of his own on arithmetic, logic, and Christian doctrine. Rome in his day had just begun to be ruled by the Ostrogoths, and the emperor Theodoric, recognizing Boethius's brilliance, eventually appointed him to be one of his highest officials (*Magister Officiorum,* roughly the equivalent of White House Chief of Staff). This, however, was the beginning of his undoing. Boethius soon ran afoul of his colleagues in court, perhaps (it seems) because he had accused some of them of corruption; they retaliated by trumping up charges of treason and sorcery against him. The charges were upheld at his trial; cruelly sentenced to die, he spent his last months in prison working on the book that would make him famous throughout Europe for centuries, *The Consolation of Philosophy*. His death sentence was carried out about a year after his arrest. The precise date of his execution and the means used are both unknown: he may have been killed by beheading with an axe or a sword, but more likely he was bludgeoned to death. He was, give or take, 45 years old at the time of his passing.

"Philosophy" in his *Consolation of Philosophy* is actually a character—a beautiful, if somewhat aging, woman who comes to console Boethius, her former student, on his impending demise. But what can Philosophy say to this relatively young man, at the height of his intellectual powers, who has been falsely accused and now faces brutal execution in a matter of months?

She finds him in his prison cell sobbing and pouring out his heart in verse (Boethius had early mastered the classical Latin meters, and he says here that poetry had been for him "the glory of a happy and verdant youth").[1] But seeing him now surrounded by the poetical Muses, Philosophy reacts with scorn: "Who gave these phony little whores access to this sick man?" she thunders. "Not only can't they provide any remedy for his suffering, but they actually keep it going with their sickly-sweet poison!" Chastened, the Muses file out, and Philosophy takes over. "What's the matter?" she then asks, turning to Boethius. "What are you crying about?" Surprised by the question, he answers, "Isn't the bitterness of fortune's cruelty reason enough?"

Philosophy then begins her consolation, which is long and complicated and in many ways still puzzles scholars. The lack of overt, Christian claims is particularly surprising in a book written by a devout Christian staring death in the face. Was Boethius an altogether cold and abstractly theoretical sort of Christian? Or, as others have suggested, did he draw a strict line between the pursuits of philosophy and theology? Or, as yet others have hinted, did he himself undergo some kind of "reverse conversion" in the face of death, abandoning Christian comfort for the unshakable, if chilly, truths of Neoplatonism?

If—for whichever reason—the book is in this sense surprisingly un-Christian, it is nonetheless, from beginning to end, rooted in the belief in God. Indeed, Philosophy starts her long discourse by cross-examining Boethius:

"Tell me, do you remember what the end of all things is, and what the whole design of nature is headed toward?"

"I used to know," I said, "but bitterness has made my memory foggy."

"Don't you know where all things come from?"

"That I do know," I said, and answered that it was God.

"Then how can it be, if you know the beginning, that you don't know the end? But such [I suppose] is the power and regular path of adversity, that it can disorient a person, even if it can't completely uproot him and separate him from himself. But I'd like you to answer this as well: do you remember that you are a man?"

"How could I not remember that?"

"Then can you explain to me what a man is?"

"Are you asking if I know myself to be a thinking and mortal creature?[2] I know and readily admit that this is what I am."

"Don't you know that you are anything else?"

"Nothing else."

"Well, now I know the other reason, the greatest one, for your sickness: you have forgotten what you are."

What Boethius is, *really* is, it turns out, is part of God's world, in which God alone is sovereign. Indeed, at the very end of the *Consolation,* in a long section dealing with human free will and divine foreknowledge, Boethius writes what was to be his dying summation of what counts in life:

"So it is not in vain that we put our hope in God and pray to Him, for when these things are done right, they cannot be without effect. So turn yourselves away from vice and practice virtue; lift your minds up to proper hopes, and offer up humble prayers to

58

Heaven. A great necessity is imposed upon you (if you don't hide from the truth): to do what is right, since whatever you do is done in the sight of a Judge who sees all things."

Boethius had little reason to lie about his beliefs; indeed, death-bed confessions are famous for their brutal honesty.* For this reason, the *Consolation of Philosophy* has always presented a particularly strong claim to represent the truth as its author actually saw it. What Boethius says he saw, even as he himself awaited unjust execution, was a world ordered by God, whom he describes as no less than an all-seeing *Judge*. But what in his own experience could possibly have made him say such a thing, *see* such a thing?

Perhaps it was nothing in his experience; perhaps it was something in his brain. This—as I came to learn later on in my reading—is the answer proposed by various neuroscientists in their own search (com-plementing that of evolutionary biologists) for some physiological basis for religious experience. Attention has focused on the "verbal conceptual association area," located at the junction of the tempo-ral, parietal, and occipital lobes of the brain. Of course, that might in any case seem like a good place to look, since religion most definitely involves a "verbal conceptual" element; but in fact experiments at UCLA conducted in the 1990s by V. S. Ramachandran demonstrated that patients with temporal lobe epilepsy are particularly sensitive to religious symbols and ideas. Subsequent experiments with nonepi-leptic volunteers have produced similar results by using an oscillat-ing magnetic field to excite temporal lobe neurons.[3] This has led to the supposition that there might be a specific spot in the brain, a "God

---

* Consider the famous last words of Ramón Narváez, duke of Valencia in the nine-teenth century; when a priest asked the duke on his deathbed if he forgave his enemies, he is reported to have replied in a somewhat embarrassed undertone, "I don't have any. I had them all shot."

spot" as it has been called, that, if stimulated (perhaps by epileptic seizure or in some other way), would lead a person to experience visions, hear divine voices, or be struck blind on the road to Damascus.

This evidence is, I suppose, open to two different interpretations. One is that all religious experience—indeed, all of religion in general—may go back to one or another incident of brain malfunction. All over the globe, according to this view, the same experience has been repeated: Some poor fellow suffers a generalized epileptic seizure—a "tonic-clonic seizure," as it is now known to physicians. The seizure often begins in a stage known to researchers as the "aura," which may last anywhere from a few minutes to some hours; at this point the seizure is relatively contained in one part of the brain, but then it gradually spreads to other parts, resulting in loss of consciousness, muscle contractions, and the other classic symptoms of epilepsy. During the "aura" phase, however, the patient is still fully conscious and often reports on intense feelings, a sense of foreboding, or, in some cases, the feeling of a "connection with an overwhelmingly powerful being," indeed, "intimate contact with an invisible God."[4] Nowadays we know a great deal about the physiology of epilepsy, but in an earlier time such seizures must regularly have been understood as real incidents of spiritual possession. Returned to his or her senses, the victim recalls the presence of that overwhelmingly powerful being, and presto! A new prophet, perhaps a whole new religion, is born.

The clinical evidence of the connection between the temporal lobe and feelings of profound religiosity certainly seemed to me suggestive, even if research following this particular line of inquiry was still at an early stage. But I mentioned that this evidence is open to different interpretations. The one given above assumes that religious experience is essentially a *malfunction,* something that goes wrong in some people's brains. But there is no logical reason for such an assumption.* Perhaps, on the contrary, what the epileptic experi-

---

* William James (*The Varieties of Religious Experience,* 1902) was already acquainted with the "epileptic" explanation, and expressed some of the same reservations: "The case of Mr. Bradley, that of M. Ratisbonne, possibly that of Colonel Gardiner, possibly

ences (and what some nonepileptics also have experienced) is not a malfunction at all, but a privileged moment, an opening of the mind to something it cannot normally perceive—perhaps something the human brain specifically evolved so as *not* to perceive, at least not most of the time—but something that is every bit as real as those parts of the light spectrum that fall outside of the range visible to the human eye, or those sound waves that make a dog's ears prick up but that our own ears are powerless to hear.

Perhaps I should enter a disclaimer at this point. I have never suffered from epilepsy or experienced the clinical symptoms just described. But they were interesting to me because of the things I *did* know, and in particular, that state of mind which is my subject in these chapters. There certainly was some area of overlap between that state of mind and what epileptics report; do they all derive from, or are they connected to, some specific thing neuroscientists can point to?

Actually, the current claim for the existence of a "God spot" in the human brain has a somewhat ironic side to it. For many centuries, ancient Hebrews, ancient Greeks, ancient Indians, and others all spoke of something inside people that they called the soul. Definitions differed, but, at the beginning at least, souls were definitely inside the body, sharing space with, or sometimes identified with, the heart, liver, kidneys, and other internal organs. Sometimes, long before the mechanics of inhalation and exhalation were understood, the soul was also said to inhabit the breath that keeps going in and out of all living creatures until their death. (The dualism of [mate-

---

that of Saint Paul, might not be so easily explained in this simple way. The result, then, would have to be ascribed either to a merely physiological nerve storm, a 'discharging lesion' like that of epilepsy; or, in case it were useful and rational, as in the two latter cases named, to some more mystical or theological hypothesis. I make this remark in order that the reader may realize that the subject is really complex. But I shall keep myself as far as possible at present to the more 'scientific' view; and only as the plot thickens in subsequent lectures shall I consider the question of its absolute sufficiency as an explanation of all the facts." See further in my next chapter.

rial] body vs. [immaterial] soul, and the physical-spiritual opposition that accompanied it, came only later on.) But eventually the concept of the soul fell into disrepute. It was still used by the French philosopher René Descartes (1596–1650), but he also spoke of the human "mind" (Latin *mens*), and it was this term that came to be preferred by later thinkers. Indeed, as the study of anatomy and human physiology developed, the soul became an object of ridicule: "Where is it?" the mockers asked. One would think that, in the light of this brief history, yesterday's mockers would today be eating crow. The soul has been found! It is in the temporal lobe of the human brain; this is where man meets God, at least when that lobe's little window somehow, sometimes, miraculously opens.

In truth, I'm not sure that I'd be prepared to sign off on this particular physiological breakthrough. I prefer the vagaries of souls in days gone by, when they were just somewhere inside us; what distinguished them from other inner organs was not their precise location, but their special connection to that which (or Him Who) is *outside* of us. This actually is the most striking, indeed, the most paradoxical aspect of the human soul as it was understood in various places in ancient times. The soul was deeply embedded *inside*, and yet it was also the doorway to the Outside, to God-who-is-emphatically-not-us.

This paradox was especially highlighted in the writings of various Jewish sages of the early postbiblical period. They liked to describe the human soul as a *pikkadón*—literally, a "deposit," something of value you might entrust to someone else to care for. The soul was God's *pikkadón,* entrusted to the human being for the duration of his or her life, but never really the person's own possession, since it was in any case slated to return to its rightful Owner after death. This situation led (not without a bit of humor) to the occasional depiction of the soul as a kind of stool pigeon. Even during our lifetimes, according to one rabbinic tradition, the soul regularly returns to God; this happens every night while we are asleep (since sleep, as a state of unconsciousness, bears witness to the soul's absence from the body). Once it has ascended on high, the soul reports to God on all the doings of the person it inhabited during the last twenty-four hours; so it is that God keeps track of humanity's good and bad deeds.

Such a conception of souls is found in an old rabbinic commentary on a verse from the biblical book of Proverbs (20:27): "A man's soul is the lamp of the LORD, searching out his innermost parts." This verse was understood in quite down-to-earth fashion: when God wants to know what someone is really thinking in "his innermost parts," He turns to the soul to go probing through that person's deepest thoughts and desires.

Rabbi Aḥa said: Just as earthly kings have detectives [*curiosi*—the Latin word for the spies or secret police regularly sent by kings to mingle with their subjects] who report everything that happens back to the king, so God too has detectives, and they tell Him all that a person does . . . The matter is comparable to the case of a man who has married the king's daughter. When, after he has gotten up in the morning, he asks the king if he is well, the king tells him each day: "You did thus and so in your house, you became angry under such and such circumstances, then you beat your servants," and so on for each and every thing. Then the man goes back and says to the members of his household: "Which of you reported that I did thus and so? How does the king know about it?" They reply: "Do not be foolish. You married his daughter and yet you ask how he knows? His own daughter tells him!" So is it with mankind: a man may do whatever he wishes, but his soul reports it back to God. (*Pesiqta Rabbati* 8)

This inside-outside paradox is no minor detail. People who believe in God generally believe (whether they know it or not) in precisely such a semipermeable membrane separating an outside Deity from an inside "me." It is thus that God (or the gods, or buddhas, "enlightened ones") can have open access to human thoughts through the agency of people's souls. This is, emphatically, what the author of Psalm 139 was reporting when he wrote:

O LORD, You search me out and know me.
You know when I am sitting around or getting up, You probe
    my thoughts from far off.
You sift my comings and goings; You are familiar with all my
    ways.
There is not one thing I say that You, LORD, do not know about.
In front and in back You press in on me and set Your hand
    on me.
Even things hidden from myself You know, things that are
    beyond me.

Where can I go from Your spirit, or how can I get away from
    You?
If I could go up to the sky, there You would be; or down to Sheol,
    there You are too.
If I took up the wings of a gull to settle at the far end of the sea,
    even there Your hand would be leading me, holding me in
    its grip.
I might think, "At least darkness can hide me, nighttime will
    conceal me."
But even darkness is not dark for You; night is as bright as the
    day, and light and dark are the same.

By the same token, God is said to speak to human beings—
theoretically any human being, but especially to prophets and sages.
In various biblical passages, He is said virtually to take over the
prophet's mind, putting His words "in the prophet's mouth" (this,
significantly, is the usual biblical idiom— not "in his ears").

To an awful lot of students of the brain, of course, such beliefs
sound nothing short of pathological. Certainly most people nowadays who "hear voices" end up lodged in institutions where they
can be kept from harming others or themselves; often the voices in
their heads can be silenced pharmacologically and their origin traced
to some chemical imbalance in the patient's brain. And yet, Juda-

ism, Christianity, Islam, and other religions all recognize prophets from an earlier day, who reported on what God had told them. By all external indication, these prophets were not madmen or madwomen (and certainly people in those ancient societies knew how to recognize insanity); most of them were stolid citizens, ranchers like Amos or temple priests like Ezekiel. How can one explain the existence of prophets back then—and their absence in our own society?

One book I read during chemotherapy was the well-known study by the experimental psychologist Julian Jaynes, *The Origin of Consciousness in the Breakdown of the Bicameral Mind* (1976). Jaynes suggested that the human brain used to function somewhat differently in ancient times (that is, up until about 3,000 years ago). He noted that, while many aspects of language and related functions are located in the two parts of the brain's left hemisphere known as Wernicke's area and Broca's area, the right-brain counterparts to these areas are nowadays largely dormant. According to Jaynes, however, those areas had been extremely important in earlier times, before humans began to perceive the world as we do now. Back then, he theorized, humans had an essentially "bicameral mind" that lacked the integrative capacities of the modern brain. Instead, its two halves functioned relatively independently: the left brain would obey what it perceived as "voices," which in fact emanated from those now-dormant areas of the right brain. (In Jaynes's formulation, the right hemisphere "organized admonitory experience and coded it into 'voices' which were then 'heard' by the left hemisphere.") Although internally generated, those voices were thus perceived by the left brain as coming from outside. It is this situation that led to the belief in communications from the gods in ancient times, as well as the belief in lesser sorts of supernatural communicators: talking spirits and genies, muses who dictated poetry to the "inspired" poet, sacred rocks, trees, and other objects that brought word "from the other side." When this bicameral mind faded out of existence and modern consciousness arose, prophecy likewise ceased and people suddenly no longer heard the gods telling them what to do.

Jaynes's theory attracted much attention when first promulgated: it answered a lot of questions in one bold stroke. But it was not long before other scholars raised significant, and eventually devastating, objections to his idea. To begin with, 3,000 years is a tiny speck of time on the scale of human evolution. How could so basic a change in the way our brains work have come about so recently? What is more, 3,000 years ago humans lived in the most varied societies and environments. Some societies were already quite sophisticated and diversified, while others then (and some still now) existed in the most rudimentary state; some humans lived in tropical forests, others in temperate climes, still others in snowy wastelands close to earth's poles; and so forth. Could human brains in these most diverse circumstances all have changed so radically at—in evolutionary terms—the same instant? Certainly now our brains all seem to function pretty much in the same way, no matter where we come from; there are no apparent surviving exemplars of the bicameral brain that Jaynes postulated. What could have caused humanity to undergo this radical change *in lockstep* all over the earth's surface? A ray from outer space?

But if Jaynes's idea has met with disapproval, the evidence he adduced is no less provocative. The problem of explaining such phenomena as the appearance and subsequent disappearance of prophecy in many societies (though certainly not all), along with the near-universal evidence of religion discussed earlier (with the widespread phenomenon of people communing with dead ancestors and/or gods—and hearing back from them), remains puzzling. Perhaps it would be better to seek a solution not in the brain's physiology, but in the whole notion of the "self" that humans carry around in their heads. For certainly one thing that scholars in many disciplines have learned is that there is nothing perfectly natural or immutable about even something as basic as the image of "me myself" through which people filter perception. Like other, less fundamental ideas we carry around in our heads—ideas about kinship (i.e., who is or is not related to you and the significance thereof); or about what sorts of

66

things you can eat and what sorts are absolutely inedible; or about the basic differences between men and women—how people in different ages and different societies conceive of "me myself" is quite variable. Of course, like these other items, a person's notion of his or her self is related to certain biological or evolutionary facts. But what the self *is* is not a fact in itself; rather, it's a way of *construing* the facts, a way of construing reality. As one scholar has observed,

> Our common-sense idea of self as some sort of entity is a human construction, in effect, virtual reality . . . Over the centuries, however, [our] belief in the existence of the self as an entity has become firmly entrenched, and it is [now] an integral part of our view of the cosmos. The point of stressing that the self is a human construction is to suggest that, as an idea, it is not inevitable.[5]

To describe the self in such terms is more than a little upsetting. After all, if there is nothing inevitable or even natural about something so basic as our sense of being a self, then what are we really? And on the other hand, if "me myself" is merely something in our minds, something that could change radically simply by our conceiving of ourselves differently, then how important can this self-image be in our actual lives? What effect can it have on our perception of objective reality? The first question is very difficult, but the other two are easy: our sense-of-self has everything to do with how we perceive reality.[6] Experimental psychologists have been aware for some time that what we think we see, for example, is very much the end result of a process of *construing* visual stimuli. More than a century ago, researchers were demonstrating this with optical illusions, and a raft of rigorous experiments have subsequently shown that our brains sometimes "correct" what our eyes report in order to make it conform to our expectations, even though our eyes are actually capturing a very different image. In one scholar's definition, vision is "the process that produces from images of the external world a description that is useful to the viewer and not cluttered with irrelevant information."[7] In an analogous way, the notion that we have of "me myself" edits and interprets our perception of reality—and as we have glimpsed already, this "me myself" is neither perfectly natural nor immutable. If we modern Westerners have our own version of the self and its relation to the outside world, this version has clearly changed since ancient times—and certainly since prehistoric times, when *Homo sapiens sapiens* first began to use the generative capacity of language for something resembling modern speech (perhaps 40,000 years ago), to manufacture more, and more sophisticated, tools and weapons, and in other ways to take on the trappings of human beings as we are today. That old "me myself" must, when you think about it, have been very different.

We can perhaps gain some sense of that old "me myself" by looking outside of our own world at other, non-Western societies or at the archaeological remains of civilizations long dead.[8] One common focus of such study has been the hunter-gatherer civilizations that flourished for millennia all over the globe (with some surviving even into modern times), since their way of life mirrors to a great extent the principal means of subsistence that prevailed for *all* people throughout most of human history.[9]

In prehistoric times people *foraged,* eating whatever they could find on trees or growing in the ground, or feeding on such living creatures as they could hunt or trap or fish (or scavenging what was left of the corpses of animals killed by other animals). Agriculture, whereby humans actively cultivate crops, as well as the domestication of animals for food, are practices that arrived relatively late in our history: the earliest evidence of agriculture goes back to only 11,000 or 12,000 years ago, when it was practiced more or less simultaneously at four or five different geographic locales, perhaps first in the Fertile Crescent of the ancient Near East. Sheep, goats, and other animals began to be domesticated for food at the same time or slightly later. But before that, for thousands and thousands of years, people just ate what they could lay their hands on, wandering from place to place in a stomach-gnawing search for food.

Hunter-gatherers in prehistoric times thus lived an uncomplicated, if perilous, existence. Most roamed about in small bands over large tracts of territory, encountering in their whole lifetime few if any humans outside the members of their own group. One such society that survived almost to the present day was that of the Aborigines of Tasmania, a large, windswept island south of Australia. Today, the Tasmanian Aborigines are no more; they quickly disappeared from their remote island's shores after the first white men began arriving in the 1820s—they were either murdered, or finished off by European diseases like bronchial pneumonia (to which they had no genetic resistance), or deported to one of various nearby islands by well-meaning reformers. Evidence of their way of life preceding their demise comes from the eyewitness accounts of early explorers as well as from archaeological findings; it has been largely pieced together in a series of studies by the archaeologist Rhys Maengwyn Jones.

The Tasmanians subsisted largely by hunting seals, red-necked wallabies (a close relative of the kangaroo), and wombats (a four-legged, furry marsupial). Seabirds such as cormorants and seagulls were also part of their diet. So were shellfish, mostly abalone and lobster, which were gathered by the Tasmanian women. (Fish had been eaten in earlier times, but for some reason the practice was abandoned long before the arrival of the Europeans.) The tools used by the Tasmanians for capturing the animals in their diet were made out of wood and stone; bone tools had been used in prehistoric times but were abandoned approximately 3,000 years ago. For hunting, the men used a long, one-piece, pliable spear sharpened at one end. All stone tools, mostly scrapers and flaked pebble choppers, were of one piece and held in the hand. The only way the Tasmanians had access to fire was to carry it on slow-burning torches wherever they went; they were incapable of making fire on their own. Jones observed that the Tasmanian repertoire of tools was "the simplest ever recorded ethnographically."[10]

The basic social unit of the Tasmanian Aborigines as observed by explorers was the "band," a small group of people who identified themselves by a particular name and which was associated with a particular piece of territory. The bands were said to "belong" to their territories, indeed, to different kinds of trees, which apparently served as totems. Each band seems to have consisted of thirty-five to forty people, a third of whom would have been children. People slept in crude huts that accommodated five to seven people. The territory that they patrolled was relatively vast for such populations—500 to 800 square kilometers inland per band; bands with waterfront territory each occupied about 25 to 35 kilometers of coastline.

The Tasmanians are only one of many hunter-gatherer societies that have been explored. In addition to studying the few exemplars still in existence, scholars have used the findings of modern archaeology to examine hunter-gatherer remains from earlier periods and places—Paleolithic and Mesolithic Europe, Siberia and northeast Asia, Australia, the Great Plains states of North America, the Andes Mountains, Australia, and other locales.[11] One thing these studies have revealed is that this general means of existence took quite varied forms in different places, and that even in one place, the hunter-gatherer society was not a static institution. Not surprisingly, as one moves back in time, the toolbox of society members becomes smaller and cruder; remains of artwork and decorative designs, telltale burial practices, and other items that might shed light on the peoples' religious ideas become simpler and fewer—and, far enough back, they disappear entirely.

It may involve some speculation, but it is not difficult for us to reconstruct at least some of what it was like to be a human in those very early days—and specifically, to reconstruct what sort of a *self* a person might have had back then. There can be little doubt that the same kind of collective self that ethnographers have identified in all sorts of non-Western societies today was simply a given for early man: he or she was part of that band, part of that totem-group, whose common foraging, scavenging existence was almost all of what life consisted of. Our early ancestors wandered about searching for food, by turns hungry or temporarily satisfied, desperate or at ease; for most, danger was never far, since human beings were still what most creatures have been since the beginning of time, simultaneously predators and someone else's potential meal.

Go back far enough and this little band of people has nothing that one could identify as *religious,* at least not in any formal sense: as noted, they bury their dead, but without grave goods; they leave behind no art or artifacts or structures such as characterize religion at a later stage. But that hardly tells the whole story. By the nature of their existence, this little group was endlessly *overshadowed* by all that was outside of them, forever on the receiving end of whatever You— immanent in the great Outside all around—happened to be dishing out. To say that their identification of You as an *agent* was the result of some "hyperactive agent detection device" is little short of ludicrous. What was the great Outside doing if not endlessly causing things to happen, as only a doer can do? On the contrary, it would require some sort of extraordinarily twisted spirit to look up and *not* see You, Your hand gloved in cloud and sky, Your voice mingling with cricket song and crashing waves, doing all the things that impinged on the little band's existence. You were practically everything, and You completely overwhelmed their own little reality. To You belonged the trees that one day budded in a nearby valley and gave them fruit; sometimes You also gave them animals to kill and eat, though sometimes not; You made the rain and then made the rain stop; You made women's bellies swell with new life; You struck down little babies and old men, killing most, though sparing some for a while. The little people controlled none of this, nor did they even think it could be understood. (I do not mean to suggest, by the way, that they conceived of You as some sort of deity—even that thought was still very far away. *You* were then just the great, undifferentiated Being who was everywhere around them, and whose reality utterly dwarfed their own.)[12]

So how, given this reality, did a single, little man's "me myself" fit into the world? Certainly it was puny; but it was also open to the great Outside, to You, in a way that modern man's is not. Long before there were gods or religion of any kind, You impinged on his existence at every turn, flowing in and out of him, making him smell this smell or think that thought, whether he liked it or not. It is really here that one should look for the semipermeable soul's beginnings.

We are different now; nowadays *we* plant the trees and raise the animals that give us food, and we know perfectly well what makes it rain and what makes women pregnant. So does not today's "me myself," even if it has been a long time in the making, have to be considered a truer version of who we really are—indeed, *the* true version? Whatever its origins and past history—in fact, precisely because of what we know of its origins—does not the semipermeable soul now look like a mistake, a misstep on the path to the true understanding of ourselves? I don't think so. The "mistake" is really in the chain of circumstances that has led to the current state of confusion in which the modern soul finds itself. *You* have remained the same; but the way we are now makes it so much harder to see.

6

"Who Shall I Say Is Calling?"

I'm still not sure how far one should take all of this. If that old sort of "me myself" was open—to the Outside, and eventually to the gods or to God—in a way that many modern human beings are not,* wasn't it also the case that death itself must have seemed different back then? Of course, death has always been fearsome, something to be opposed with all one's might: surely human beings, like other animals, have always fought with tooth and nail to preserve their own lives. But in so doing, have the humans always conceived of what they were doing in the way we do now when, for example, we die of a cerebral hemorrhage or a cancerous tumor discovered in the large intestine? Or was there a time when we were much smaller, so that even our ceasing-to-exist was never a merely internal affair, but rather a matter of being *struck down* by outside forces, perhaps by hostile powers or perhaps merely by a timely kiss from the Angel of Death—but, whatever the precise form and circumstances, in a way that made our death part of a larger picture?

In fact, when someone nowadays really *knows* he's dying, doesn't he revert, at least a little bit, to that old way of seeing things? (This certainly was part of what I getting at in the first chapter about the

---

* I don't mean that we are all, or even mostly, unbelievers, only that the character of our belief is altogether different from this ancient way of seeing.

music stopping.) For most of our lives, the idea of death is there, but only as an idea, abstract and distant. But then, for at least some people, the day arrives when it suddenly becomes something very, very concrete. Then death at last steps out of the shadows, standing in the sunlight, undisguised.

I hesitated for a while about the title of this book. The biblical verse it alludes to probably did not mean what the King James translators thought it meant, "Yea, though I walk through the valley of the shadow of death." To begin with, in the ancient Near East—unlike most of Europe or America—"shadow" generally had no negative connotations. The sun was hot, sometimes fatally so; *shade* or *shadow* saved you from its dangers. These words therefore generally had positive associations; often they were used metaphorically for "protection." So the *shadow of death* just doesn't ring true. Besides, it's not even clear that there are two nouns here. They appear here and elsewhere in the Bible as a single word, *salmawet* or perhaps *salmut*, which seems simply to be a synonym of "darkness," without any connection to death. Hence the translation of our verse as found in many modern Bibles, "Even though I walk through the darkest valley . . ."

But if "the valley of the shadow of death" is a mistranslation, it's still a very evocative phrase since, for most people most of the time, that's what death is, something shadowy that we push to the back of our minds. It's always there, but only as an idea, abstract and distant. But then suddenly, one day, it's not. All at once it is clear to you that this is pretty much it—nothing fancy, just the end. At that moment, isn't your modern, Western self necessarily transformed, *contracted* into something different from what it has been?

The matter of where a person's interior self ends and the Outside begins was an issue that presented itself in the most down-to-earth terms to the British anthropologist Godfrey Lienhardt (1921–1993) when he set out to study the Dinka people of southern Sudan. In their religion, Lienhardt reported, the Dinka recognize different kinds of divine "Powers," spirits and clan-divinities as well as divine beings associated with various features of the natural world—wood, streams, lightning, and so forth.[1] Not all of the Powers are beneficent, he was told: some are responsible for disease or spirit possession.

> Traditional teaching affirms the existence of Powers and endows them with some of their specific characteristics; but their effective relationship with men at particular times, in the direct encounters which make them so much more vividly present to the Dinka than they can be to ourselves, are matters to be discovered . . . by divining and questioning.[2]

Through magical divination as well as an examination of the people and events involved, the precise identity of the malevolent Power afflicting someone could—the Dinka told Lienhardt—usually be determined.

However—and this is my point in citing from his study—Lienhardt found that he faced a particularly perplexing problem in trying to describe *how* the Dinka view these Powers' activity affecting a human being. The Dinka have, he concluded, a very different sense of the human self. For that reason, describing how an outside Power acts on people

> raises first a difficult question of differences between Dinka and European self-knowledge, which I can discuss only inadequately. The Dinka have no conception which at all closely corresponds to our popular, modern conception of the "mind" as mediating and, as it were, storing up the experiences of the self. There is for them no such interior entity to . . . stand between the experiencing self at any given moment and what is or has been an exterior influence upon the self.
>
> So it seems that what we should call the "memories" of experi-

ences, and regard therefore as in some way intrinsic and *interior* to the remembering person and modified in their effect upon him by their interiority, appear to the Dinka as *exteriorly* acting upon him . . . Hence it would be impossible to suggest to a Dinka that a powerful dream was "only" a dream, and might for that reason be dismissed as relatively unimportant in the light of day; or that a state of possession was grounded "merely" in the psychology of the person possessed. *They do not make the kind of distinction between the psyche and the world . . .*

A man who had been imprisoned in Khartoum called one of his children "Khartoum" in memory of the place, but also to turn aside any possible harmful influence of that place upon him in later life. The act is an act of exorcism, but the exorcism of what, for us, would be memories of experiences . . . [T]he power which has once affected a man . . . or the places which have formed a man's personality, are regarded as potent still to affect him, as they once certainly affected him, directly, and from without . . .

Even in the usual expressions of the Dinka for the action of features of their world upon them, we often find a reversal of European expressions, which assume the human self, or mind, as subject in relation to what happens to it. In English, for example, it is often said that a man "catches a disease," but in Dinka the disease, or Power, always "seizes" the man.[3]

What Lienhardt seems to be getting at is not merely the fact that the Dinka live in a world populated by divine "outside" forces that act on people, but what this view of things seems to say about their own notion of self. They don't have our kind of self, that is, the ongoing, interior entity that is all that we Westerners think of as our own, irreducible "me," the sum total of all the characteristics that we possess and the things that we have done or experienced and therefore are. Instead, "There is for them no such interior entity to . . . stand between the experiencing self at any given moment" (that is, the immediate, unadorned being who is simply there, being acted upon by whatever is happening) "and what is or has been an *exterior* influence upon the self."

All this is, I think, connected to what we now recognize as the highly variable point in the human mind where an interior "I" leaves off and the outside world begins. Neuroscientists and other researchers know well that the inside-outside divide that we generally walk around with ("I am the person inside my body") is, when you get down to it, merely a construct. As one scholar has written:

> The naïve boundary between "me" and the "outside world" is my skin (and the lenses of my eyes), but, as we learn more and more about the way events in our own bodies can be inaccessible "to us," the great outside encroaches. "In here" I can try to raise my arm, but "out there," if it has "fallen asleep" or is paralyzed, it won't budge; my lines of communication from wherever *I* am to the neural machinery controlling my arm have been tampered with. And if my optic nerve were somehow severed, I wouldn't expect to go on seeing, even though my eyes were still intact. Having visual experiences is something that apparently happens *inboard* of my eyes, somewhere in between my eyes and my voice when I tell you what I see.[4]

By the same token, if "I" am in charge of "in here," then why can't I order those little cancer cells to stop reproducing? For that matter, why can't I turn off my graying hair and wrinkles and other signs of aging? Why can't *I* stop killing *me*? Looked at from this perspective, it began to seem as if "I" is really just some sort of front man, a distraction invented (by whom?) to allow the chaos of different inputs and cellular instructions to go their merry, heedless way.

All this is connected to what neuroscientists and other theoreticians call "the problem of consciousness" and a mystery that might be summarized by the phrase used everywhere by secretaries answering their bosses' telephones, "Who shall I say is calling?" When it comes to the brain, scientists really don't know. It would be nice to be able to identify the brain's real command center and so find out who we are dealing with, digging through all those layers of sense perceptions and memories and whatever else is there in order to get down to the real root of our being—like clearing a desk of its piles of accumulated notes and papers to get down to just Plain Flat, the "me myself" on top of which everything else is piled. But, in the end, just Plain Flat may not exist.

In an earlier day, the command center of the human being was often thought to be located not in the brain, but in the heart. This idea had a certain logic to it; the heart is centrally located, it seems to beat faster when things get exciting, and perhaps most significantly, when the heart stops beating, the person (or animal) stops living. In ancient Semitic languages (and no doubt others), the heart was thus identified as the place of human thought. But even after attention came to focus on the brain,[5] it was simply assumed that the brain *as a whole* was the human command center. That is, the eyes, the ears, the nose, and other senses reported to the brain, which then commanded the hands, the fingers, or the feet to react in this or that fashion. With time, however, scientists began to realize that the brain wasn't one, single, unified entity. Part of it was devoted to making sense of images carried from the eyes; part to sorting out sounds carried from the ears and smells from the nose; another part to touch, temperature, and pain; yet other parts controlled body movements; then there was the whole autonomic nervous system; and on and on and on. Moreover, it turned out that it wasn't just that "outside" stimuli reached the brain, where they were sorted, catalogued, and reacted to. The brain itself turned out to be a *creator* of reality, so that a lot of what seemed to be "out there" turned out to be happening "in here." (Needless to say, this has the most profound implications for the semipermeable soul.)

But if so, who's in charge "in here"—and can that entity really be credibly identified as "me"? At first scholars thought that there had to be a command center *within the brain* to synthesize all the different functions exercised by the frontal lobe, parietal lobe, occipital lobe, and so forth—a command center to coordinate all this activity in order to be able to tell the limbs, the lungs, and so forth what to do. That would be the real "me," telling every other part of the brain (and in turn, the body) what to do. Descartes was convinced that this command center was none other than the pineal gland, a pea-sized little body that sits between the two hemispheres of the brain near its very center; for him it was nothing less than *le siège de l'âme* (the seat of the soul). This too looked like a reasonable hypothesis; a command center ought to be located somewhere in the brain's midsection. But modern medicine has proven Descartes' theory wrong. The pineal gland exercises no such role; its main function in humans seems to be the production of melatonin, the hormone that regulates sleep.

So what *is* the brain's command center? The extremely disturbing conclusion of some neuroscientists today is that no such center exists. Somehow, in a way that is difficult to translate into an understandable model, our brains succeed in working without one. As one clinician has eloquently summed up the problem:

> When the self is considered from the standpoint of neuroscience, one primary concern is how awareness is integrated and organized into a coherent whole, since that *whole* is what is emphasized when we refer to "the self" or "the mind." Here the emphasis is not upon any single momentary act of perception or motor response, but rather upon the totality of the brain's functions into unified experience and action. Indeed, one major reason why the self seems so difficult to explain on a purely neurobiological basis is that, while we experience a unified consciousness, there appears to be an essential difference between the unified mind and the divisible brain. We know the nervous system is composed of millions of neurons grouped into numerous larger structures. The question is, how do all these physically connected but materially separable

79

structures function as a seamless whole that we experience as our unified selves?[6]

It may be that our brains are constantly busy revising and reimagining reality as new input enters, so that (in the words of another theorist) "all varieties of perception—indeed, all varieties of thought or mental activity—are accomplished in the brain by parallel, multitrack processes of interpretation and elaboration of sensory inputs." In other words, information keeps entering the brain and keeps being re-construed through a process of "continuous editorial revision,"[7] with one "draft" endlessly replacing another in response to new stimuli. This *is* hard to imagine, and that may be a good reason to suppose that neuroscience still has a way to go before "Who shall I say is calling?" has a satisfactory answer.

Part of that way may be shown by our own thinking machines. Since the dawn of the computer age, the human mind has been compared to the workings of a computer, and a subset of computer science has long been devoted to trying to build a machine that can reproduce the phenomenon of consciousness in semiconductors and copper wiring. Theoretically, at least, it ought to be possible; human beings are, after all, *material*—our bodies and our brains are made up of living cells; can't all this be duplicated through modern technology? So far, however, that goal has proven elusive. Scientists can devise computer programs that have sophisticated rules governing responses to varied input (they can thus "teach" a computer to play chess and even defeat a grand master), but the dream of building a *conscious* robot, one that has its own "me myself" and thinks independently and *feels* the way we do, seems almost as fantastic as it did centuries ago, when the sixteenth-century Maharal of Prague (Rabbi Yehudah Loew b. Bezalel) was reported to have used his esoteric knowledge to build a golem, a sentient human being, out of clay.

Even if we can't build a conscious robot, what is known today about the brain can be compared in some respects to the way a computer works. Like a computer, our brains are material entities, and on this physical level, we know perfectly well the materials out of which a human brain is fashioned, as well as how it "works" through synapses and neurons (in the same way that we know how a computer works via electricity moving through wires and then being channeled into and through the machine). Beyond these physical facts comes the second level, the configuration of this raw material and basic functioning into the brain's equivalent of the computer's hardware—motherboard, RAM (random-access memory), logic gates, microchips, and so forth. This can hardly be said to be fully understood today, although neuroscientists know a lot more than they used to. But then comes yet a third level of analysis, still less well known, which might be compared to the computer's full array of software. How do different "programs," all running at once, interact with each other to produce what we call consciousness? If there is no command center, what exactly are we doing by using the pronoun "I"? Here, scientists are still very much in the dark.

O felix incognitum—what a breakthrough! Because, of course, this does shine a somewhat different light on what people are doing when they think about God, an act that (as I have been maintaining) has so much to do with how they conceive of themselves, that elusive "I." Is not our modern way of seeing, or not seeing, very much tied to the sealed-off self that we now construe, a somewhat different organ from the semipermeable soul it has replaced? Some theorists may say that God is a human construct, but doesn't it change things to realize that the first construct is the constructor himself?

> *Scene on a puppet stage: an elaborate medieval castle. Princess Plain*
> *Flat, all gauze and pointy hat, comes riding up to the gates. Knock*
> *knock knock knock knock.*
> "Yes?"
> "I want to see the King."

"Certainly. Who shall I say is calling?"

"Princess Plain Flat."

"Who?"

"Princess Plain Flat."

"Who?"

"Princess . . . Plai-Fla . . ."

"Who?"

"Pri . . . Pri-pla-fluh . . ."

"Who?"

"Puhh . . . Pruh . . . Prupple-affle . . ."

"Excellent. The King will see you now."

In Boethius's time, "philosophy" played a role similar to what we call science in our own day. Philosophy wasn't just vague speculation, but the most rigorous way of trying to understand the world that people could come up with, relying as it did on the immutable laws of mathematics and geometry and logic, as well as on all that could be deduced by careful observation. In fact, I think the reason why Boethius wrote his book the way he did—devoid of anything that might smack of Christian dogma or even (as he believed) anything that depended on unverifiable faith—was because he wanted above all just to understand, to know the truth, via the best science of his day. The question that he had was not, "Why is this happening to me? I've been a good Christian," but "Why this disorder, this apparent randomness in the world's operation?" The prospect of near-certain death a little more than halfway through the (even then) normal human life span of seventy or eighty years had to have some explanation. How could this square with "the facts" as he knew them? After all, God made the world and continues to micromanage it, day by day, and God is unquestionably good . . .

The first thing that Philosophy tells him is rather shocking: it all has to do with Fortuna. Fortuna was an ancient Roman goddess, a somewhat capricious deity responsible for the vicissitudes of national and personal life. As a Christian, Boethius could not suggest that she was an actual goddess, but he plays on this old tradition to talk about lowercase *fortuna,* "luck" or "chance," as if it were a "she" and an actual force in the world. Philosophy asks him,

> What is it, O human, that has thrown you into sadness and strife? You think you've seen something new and unusual: you think fortune has changed the way she treats you? You're wrong. That's the way she always acts—it's her nature . . . So now you have discovered the changeable countenance of this blind deity; she may have hidden herself from others up until now, but you, at least, have come to know her completely. So if you approve of her, then accept the way she acts and don't complain. But if you detest her treachery, then cast her off along with her harmful delusions.

Those "delusions" consist of all the superficial goods of this world—fame and fortune, power and glory, even health and long life—in short, all the things that most people believe to be important. They are handed out or taken back as fortune determines—in fact, losing them is inevitable. So, Philosophy tells Boethius, since you accepted them unreflectively when fortune was treating you well, it really makes no sense that you should start asking questions now. The only alternative to being treated and mistreated by fortune is to realize that true happiness—what Boethius calls "blessedness"—is not to be found in any of the things that fortune gives or takes back. "Blessedness" is within each person. "So why, mortals, should you go looking for happiness outside, when it has been placed inside of you?"

I'm not sure how persuasive Philosophy's words of consolation— much of them a straightforward restatement of classical Stoic think-ing—would seem to most people in the twenty-first century, or even how they struck most of Boethius's contemporaries. If the problem of evil were so easily solved, the lines already quoted would no doubt be a catechism of every religious faith. But since there is no solution, I think what made for much of the appeal of Boethius's book over the course of the next ten centuries was its author's honesty. Listen to this later exchange between him and Philosophy:

"No one can doubt," she said, "that God is all-powerful."

"Whoever is of sound mind," I said, "can hardly waffle about that."

"Thus, for Someone who is all-powerful," she said, "there is nothing He cannot do."

"Certainly not," I said.

"And yet, is God capable of doing evil?"

"Not at all," I said.

"Therefore," she said, "evil must be nothing, since He who is all-powerful cannot do it."

"Are you kidding me?" I asked . . .

I began reading about neuroscience in the middle of my treatment because—a bit like Boethius, I suppose—I wanted to console myself not with comforting creeds but, somewhat perversely perhaps, with "just the facts" as best they can be known. And certainly the neuroscientist's path to understanding religion, like the evolutionary biologist's, seems full of promise. As humans developed as a species, it was not only their bodies that evolved, but their minds and patterns of behavior. These simply became—like the capacity for speech, indeed, like the physical makeup of those parts of the brain preprogrammed for speech and colors and right vs. wrong—part of what a human being was, or rather, *is*. But it is this "is" that has ended up being the most problematic part of the whole modern discussion. Now that we may be beginning to understand something about what has gone into making us into a religious species, the question that this research has raised for many is: what is to be the effect of this knowledge on how we live henceforth?

As I look at my own mini-library of recent books in this field, I can't escape the feeling that the authors of most of these studies have somehow misconstrued what their research is all about. Something like a missionary fervor is carried in their very titles, *Breaking the Spell* and *The God Delusion* and *Virus of the Mind* and *Rethinking Religion* and *In Gods We Trust* and *Religion Explained.* They all seem to be saying: once we understand the neuroscience and evolutionary biology that explain how this delusion got going in the first place, then we can start to come to our senses and reorder our lives. But that really *is* to miss the whole point. It's the equivalent of saying that once evolutionary biologists have fully explained the forces responsible for the particular characteristics of human courtship behavior, and once neuroscientists can tell us exactly how our brains have been shaped to create the various neural interactions that foster attraction between males and females of reproductive age, then we can at last stop falling in love and reconfigure the business of mate selection on purely scientific grounds; then the money now squandered on such foolishness as lipstick and other cosmetics, beautiful clothes and fast cars and bodybuilding equipment and expensive restaurants can be poured into more socially useful activities. What nonsense! Surely there is a difference between trying to understand human behavior—including, perhaps especially including, the things we feel most keenly in the fiber of our being—and using such explanations in order to redesign something that is a basic part of what it means to be human (as these very studies have shown!).

Beyond this rather obvious point, however, stands that disputed fault line that separates "inside" from "outside" in humans, and everything about it that we still do not understand. Clearly, this has a great deal to do with the world of the soul and what it sees. And so it does no good to say, as some of those books do, "Since God is demonstrably not an old man with a white beard who controls the world, therefore all religion is nonsense"; this is to make things a little too easy for religion's debunkers. After all is said and done, it may come down to a choice between seeing something real through a wavy lens—precisely at the aforementioned inside-outside divide—and not seeing at all. Faced with such a choice, I'll take seeing anytime.

But even that doesn't quite say it all for me. There is something about that first title mentioned, *Breaking the Spell,* that begs to be reversed. Because really, who is it that lives under a greater spell, the fervent African animist communing with a sacred tree or the average modern American going about his or her daily routine? I don't mean this as a snipe at American society, and certainly not at our whole way of looking into things scientifically—I have the greatest regard for science, if for no other reason than that it saved me from dying at the age of 55 or 56. Nor is this observation intended to evoke the great Romantic tradition of exalting the noble savage. Rather, what I have in mind is what I have been calling our peculiar way of fitting into the world. There is something profoundly weird about the way we in the modern West conceive of ourselves, or rather, *don't* conceive of ourselves, as we shuffle through our days. The African animist is not a philosopher, but he does have a definite advantage in this very basic matter of fitting into the world. To return to that old-fashioned word, I think it ultimately comes down to two differently configured souls: his is still vibrant and fundamentally open, while ours has become a strangely stunted and sealed organ, the product of the harsh environment in which it has been forced to develop. This is really what needs to be better understood if we are to assess our own way of life.

All this is me talking now, but it wasn't exactly how I saw things then. What I remember about then is finding these ideas interesting, but also altogether disconnected from the world I was in. That world was much more basic, down to fundamentals: holding on. The utter reality of it . . . *Ideas* about God seemed a funny luxury. No need then to think about what was real. What was real was this afternoon: no soft curves, just squares and rectangles rubbing up against each other with great friction, raw ... And, forgive me if I say it again, the smallness—trying to live among the great elements of the present, wife and children, afternoon sun, the starkness of the late-autumn afternoon sun.

7

Into the Stark World

I tried to keep writing that book I had started, but some days the chemotherapy drugs were just too powerful. I would get up, get dressed, and start the day, but then after about an hour, I would find myself back in the bedroom, lying on top of the covers, too exhausted even to hold a book. Talk radio is boring, so I eventually went back to the music I had listened to thirty years earlier: Bob Dylan, Leonard Cohen. One day, I put on an album by Judy Collins. The last cut was her a cappella version of the old Protestant hymn "Amazing Grace." Listening to it, I was struck by the stark, abstract quality of the words. Here there were no nuances, no subtle shades of meaning:

> Amazing grace! how sweet the sound,
> That saved a wretch like me!
> I once was lost but now am found,
> Was blind, but now I see.

I had heard these words before, but they never struck me the way they did now. Why is it that religious poetry is so often abstract and stark in this way? Those writers live in the same world as other human beings, but it obviously looks very different to them. Suddenly, everything is reduced to essences, polar opposites: lost/found, blind/see. For some reason, this very much resonated with my own state of mind at the time.

I suppose this is the case with many people who are seriously ill. I don't mean to say that they suddenly become what some Americans like to call "spiritual," or even just desperate. Rather, it's that the concrete here-and-now becomes their whole existence. The stiff, white feel of your hospital pillowcase is now a major element of reality, along with the shiny glare coming off the pastel green wall facing your hospital bed. Your eyes keep closing and then opening again onto the same scene. People come and go—nurses, doctors, your family, a friend or two. They talk to you through a thick wall of imaginary Plexiglas, sometimes with emphatic gestures or great guffaws to make sure you understand. Most of it is make-talk talk, in which you try to help out as best you can; then, "Well, I'll let you get some rest." Rest? You live in a world of rest. On the other side of your window, outside reality is going on like some bizarre movie. Are those really cars parked on the flat roof of the adjoining building? How did they get up there?

In the "stark" mind-set, it is as if our very sense of sight, all those subtle shapes and shades, becomes treacherous and unreliable. Real reality is elsewhere, deep in the soul, in a land of primary colors and yes-or-no. Those corny titles of the TV evangelists—"Hour of Decision," "Night of Hope"—express well this new, all-or-nothing feel that life has for you. So too do the album covers of collections of gospel music: the lonely little man sits on a bench in a black room, while a great beam of light shoots down through a high window. I remember lying on my bed and wondering about this part of my state of mind—and about the person who wrote "Amazing Grace." I promised myself that, if I ever felt better, I would get up and go to the library and find out who he was and what made him write it.

John Newton was born in England in 1725. His mother died when he was only six, and his father, a sea captain, clearly had no idea what to do with him. After a time he sent his son off to boarding school, where he remained for two years; his father then took him out of school at the age of eleven in order to have him join him on a series of sea voyages. John thus learned his father's trade at an early age, and he was subsequently inducted into naval service. But the young man did not take to the discipline of that way of life. He eventually jumped ship, was punished, and then found work on a slave-trading vessel. Far from objecting to this commerce in human misery, John Newton actually took to it—and got rich in the process.

He later liked to say that his great conversion experience took place on March 10, 1748, the day when, during his return voyage to England, a storm came up and nearly sank the ship he was on; he found himself suddenly crying out, "Lord, have mercy upon us," and the ship was saved. If so, however, the effects of this experience took a while to work themselves out. Newton continued to work in the slave trade for some time, and, although he sought to reform his life somewhat, by his own admission he only became a "believer" in the full sense of the word much later on. In 1755 he left off seafaring for good and, while working in Liverpool, began to study Greek and Hebrew, the two languages of Scripture; after some difficulties, he was ordained as an Anglican priest in 1764. A charismatic preacher, he attracted many followers as curate of Olney (Buckinghamshire); it was there that he wrote the hymn now known as "Amazing Grace," which he published in the *Olney Hymns* in 1779. Although presented there as a kind of meditation on 1 Chronicles 17:16 ("Who am I, O LORD God, and what is my family, that You have brought me thus far? . . ."), the song is in a real sense Newton's own autobiography. In that same year, 1779, he was invited to serve as rector of the famous Saint Mary Woolnoth church in London, where he remained until his death in December of 1807.

Thus, despite the all-or-nothing, black-or-white world of "Amazing Grace," Newton's life seems to have been rather like most people's. His conversion may have begun, as he reports, in 1748, but he must have thought about the event and mulled it over for some years before it began to have any impact on his way of life. (Indeed, a skeptical biographer might even wonder whether the incident Newton described was a flash of insight, or if rather, like a great many people, Newton "rewrote" his life history in his own mind to conform to what he later became.) In any case, one might rightly ask about Newton's version of his own life the same question that arises from "Amazing Grace": why these polar opposites? That isn't how life is for most people, and it does not seem as if that was the way it really was for him. So is this starkness just a willful distortion, or perhaps a convention? No hypothesis is to be lightly discarded. But starkness seems to be too basic, and too widespread, a feature of religious perception to be dismissed as artifice.

To begin with, it is all over the Bible. Numerous psalms, for example, describe a world stripped down to the essential, right and wrong, good and evil, following God or going astray. It is a theme that, apparently, cannot be stressed enough:

> The Lord's teaching is perfect, restoring one's life;
> the Lord's decrees are enduring, making the simple wise.
> The Lord's ordinances are straight, causing one's heart to rejoice.
> What the Lord commands is clear, bringing enlightenment to
>   the eye.
> The fear of the Lord is pure, lasting forever.
> The Lord's judgments are true, righteous altogether,
> more desirable than gold, than the finest gold, in fact.
> They are sweeter than honey, the drippings of the honeycomb.
> Indeed, Your servant is guided by them; great is the reward for
>   keeping them. (Psalm 19)

> For God alone my soul silently waits; my hope comes from Him.
> He alone is my rock and deliverance, the fortress from whom I
>   will not stray . . .
> On God my survival and my honor depend; my strong rock and
>   shelter is in God.

Trust in Him at all times, O people; pour out your hearts before
　　Him; God is our shelter. (Psalm 62)

Raise a shout for God, all the earth! Sing the glory of His name,
　　make glorious His praise!
Say of God, "How fearsome are Your doings! Your enemies
　　cower before Your great strength.
The whole earth bows down before You and sings Your praises,
　　singing praise to Your name." (Psalm 66)

But how can a fellow straighten his way and follow Your words?
I have begged You with my whole heart, do not let me stray from
　　Your commandments.
Deep in my heart I have buried what You said, so that I not sin
　　against You.
Blessed are you, O LORD; teach me Your laws.
By myself I have recited all of Your rules.
I like better the path of Your statutes than any riches.
Let me speak some of Your precepts and behold Your paths.
I take pleasure in Your laws. Let me bear Your words in mind.
　　(Psalm 119)

All this sometimes comes close to sounding like propaganda; is it
really what the psalmist saw—was everything so clear-cut, so simple? But it is not just the book of Psalms. Another, somewhat less
frequently read biblical book is Proverbs. There, all of humanity
is regularly divided into two groups, the righteous (or, in modern
English, the "good") and the wicked (the "bad").

No harm befalls the righteous, but the wicked are full of
　　misfortune. (Proverbs 12:21)

The house of the wicked will be destroyed, but the tent of the
　　upright will flourish. (Proverbs 14:11)

The LORD is far from the wicked, but He hears the prayer of the
righteous. (Proverbs 15:29)

"No harm befalls the righteous"—in what world did the author
of those words live? And how can it be that the average Joe has absolutely no place in this book's vision of things—is there really no one
on earth who is neither altogether good nor altogether bad? But deep
in the soul, it seems, there are no middling, so-so answers: it really is
a place of all or nothing.

Behold, I set before you this day a blessing and a curse. The blessing, if you obey the commandments of the LORD your God, which
I am commanding you today; and the curse, if you do not obey the
commandments of the LORD your God, but turn from the path
that I am commanding you today and follow other gods who have
not been your own . . .
I call heaven and earth today to witness concerning you: life and
death I am setting before you, the blessing and the curse. Choose
life, so that you may live, devoted to the LORD your God, obeying
and clinging to Him. (Deuteronomy 11:26–28; 30:19)

Later Judaism continued this stark vision. Among its many expressions, I have always liked the famous metaphorical description of
human life attributed to Rabbi Akiba (ca. 50–135 C.E.):

Everything is given on pledge, and a net is spread over all the living. The shop is open for business, and the shopkeeper sells on
credit; the account books are open and the hand is writing, and
anyone who wants to borrow is welcome to do so. But the collectors make their rounds steadily every day, and they collect a man's
debts whether he knows it or not—and they have a solid basis for
what they do. So the judgment is fair—and everything has been
prepared for a feast. (m. *Abot,* 3:16)

I suppose the basic idea is clear enough: God's world is like an old-fashioned neighborhood grocery store, into which anyone can go and buy whatever he or she wants on credit. But the starkest element in this description is the one that really doesn't fit with the overall shop metaphor, "and a net is spread over all the living." Some have suggested that this is a biblical allusion (Ecclesiastes 9:12), but I doubt it. I think it is just a general assertion (and a rather ominous one at that): wherever you go and whatever you do, every little thing is taking place in an enclosed space; everyone is trapped under God's huge net. You don't see the net, of course—your eyes are no guide in this— but it is there nonetheless. So people are certainly free to do whatever they want, but all the while "the account books are open and the hand is writing," and sooner or later every debt (a frequent image of sin in both Judaism and Christianity)[1] will have to be paid back. In fact, those "collectors" pass through the population unobserved, and the little accidents of life, the mishaps that befall all of us, are really all the collectors' work; we keep paying back whether we like it or not, whether we are even aware of it or not.

This is, of course, a rather frightening picture of life: it would seem (to switch metaphors) that we're given an unlimited quantity of rope with which to hang ourselves. Perhaps that is why the passage ends on a more optimistic note, asserting that the collectors "have a solid basis for what they do," and that the judgment is fair; in fact, "everything has been prepared for a feast," presumably in the next world. But this assertion in no way diminishes the overall aura of starkness: yes or no, black or white, you can't see God's net because it isn't part of the visible world. In any case, that world really doesn't count; it's this other, invisible one that is important, and it is ticking every minute of the day.

I would chalk up to the same mentality those magnificent works of medieval art and architecture in Western Europe: they too inhabit a spiritual world that is far from the everyday. When modern museum-goers first encounter medieval paintings, most react with incomprehension and not a little distaste: "Why didn't these people learn how to draw?" Bodies that seem to belie the most elementary facts of human anatomy, little children who actually look like full-grown adults shrunk down to 30 percent of their normal size, Christ and various angels that seem to look like ordinary human beings in every respect save for their uncanny capacity for midair suspension—what's going on here? But these, too, are a product of the stark world. What is interesting about humans, the artists seem to say, is not their physical existence; what you see in my painting is merely a projection of their spiritual significance into a world of basically irrelevant physical forms. For the same reason, God Himself sits in heaven fully embodied, an ordinary man: it's all taking place in the supernal realms anyway. There, haloes are everyday headgear, and the background is awash in heraldry; everything contains a symbolic message.

Gothic cathedrals belong to the same world. Later on, in the Renaissance, the human form and the average person's height would shape the architect's vision; courtyards and open spaces would, at the same time, frame the church's exterior and, as it were, put it into perspective. But in medieval times, the church was to be, on the contrary, a place of God's overwhelming, stark presence. So the columns inside rose to impossible heights, dwarfing worshipers as they stood meekly below; flying buttresses supported huge, broken-arched ceilings, which seemed by their very construction to reach, no, to *be* the heights of heaven. Here the faithful might come and actually enter God's world, a place of absolutes in which man was very small and definitely not the measure of all things.

It has always seemed to me that early Christians read the Bible in the same stark way. Nowadays, that old way of reading has been largely abandoned (although traditional Jewish interpretation of the Bible, out of which Christian interpretation first developed, is still very much alive). Today's Christians—at first it was only the Protestants, but in the mid-twentieth century Roman Catholics joined in—largely focus on the straightforward meaning of the words, aided by our sophisticated knowledge of biblical Hebrew and Greek as well as of the historical circumstances in which the various books of the Bible came into existence (and quite divorced from ancient traditions of interpretation). But in an earlier age, that was not how the Bible was read. The straightforward meaning of the words was downplayed, since, in that ancient hermeneutic, every word could always have some symbolic or typological meaning—"Jerusalem" could mean "my soul," for example, and "Israel" could mean "the Church" or "one who sees God." The real-world events apparently being recounted in Scripture were also basically ciphers, symbols of events that take place in the spiritual realm. The Israelites' crossing of the Red Sea may have really happened, but for early Christians, it represented something else: the defeat of Satan, and the efficacy of baptism in overcoming sin. This was another way of saying that the events that the eyes see, or that are reported in the literal sense of Scripture, are merely a distraction: real reality is elsewhere.

Such was the Bible of the early Church's interpreters: Clement, Origen, Augustine, and those who succeeded them. I have always liked that passage in Augustine's *Confessions* in which he describes his reaction to reading the Bible for the first time. The actual text of the Bible that he was reading—we are in the late fourth century c.e.—was not the later, mellifluous Latin translation known as the Vulgate, but a much clumsier, awkward version now studied only by scholars, the *Vetus Latina*. Whoever was responsible for this translation was apparently not much of a stylist, and his work even contained a few glaring grammatical errors. Augustine's initial reaction was thus to find the text rather repugnant. But in reliving that moment, he also reveals something about the way he later came to feel about the Bible:

So I made up my mind to examine the Holy Scriptures and see what kind of books they were. I discovered something that was at

97

once beyond the understanding of the proud and hidden from the eyes of children. Its gait was humble, but the heights it reached were sublime. It was enfolded in mysteries, but I was not the kind of man to enter into it or bow my head to follow where it led. But these were not the feelings I had when I first read the Scriptures . . . I had too much conceit to accept their simplicity and not enough insight to penetrate their depths. It is surely true that as the child grows, these books grow with him. But I was too proud to call myself a child. I was puffed up with self-esteem, which made me think myself a great man. (3:5)

The stark Bible was indeed "enfolded in mysteries"; the actual words were only flickering clues as to the text's real meaning, and the shabby outward appearance of the Bible's Latin was (what a striking image!) like a small, rude door that, once traversed, opened onto a palace of sublime heights. In other words, real reality is not what our eyes report to our brains; those externals only distract us from what is actually taking place. But seeing that rude door for the first time, Augustine says, "I was not the kind of man to enter into it or bow my head to follow where it led." A bit later, he expands on this same theme:

But You, O God, whom I love and on whom I lean in weakness so that I may be strong, You are not the sun and the moon and the stars, even though we see these bodies in the heavens; nor are You those other bodies which we do not see in the sky, for You created them [as well] and in your reckoning, they are not even among the greatest of Your works.[2] How far, then, must You really be from those fantasies of mine, those imaginary material things which do not exist at all! The images we form in our mind's eye, when we picture things that really do exist, are far better founded than these inventions; and the things themselves are still more certain than the images we form of them. But You are not these things . . . Where were You in those days? How far away from me? . . . I tried to find You, not through the understanding of the mind, by which You meant us to be superior to animals, but through the fleshly senses. Yet You were deeper than my inmost understanding and higher than the highest height that I could reach.

The "fleshly senses," Augustine says, are an illusion, and even the "images we form in our mind's eye" fall short of the reality of God. What is truly going on in the world, like what is truly going on in Scripture, has little to do with the apparent, superficial significance.

It may seem an irreverent comparison at this point, but the same relationship that exists between medieval and Renaissance art and thought exists as well in movie theaters. Regular films have nothing to do with starkness: they are all about *our* world and the way things normally look. But animated cartoons are another story: their bright, primary colors and abstract spirituality fit perfectly with starkness, as does their utter disdain for "real reality." There is nothing like the real, external world in cartoons, nothing of the sunlight and shadow that is "out there." What is so clever about cartoons is that they merely *seem* to represent that outside world, whereas what they actually show takes endless delight in breaking the outside world's rules. Like Augustine's Bible, the resemblance to ordinary reality is merely the starting point, a representation that, soon enough, will turn out to be different from what one might think. So the sun, if it appears at all in a cartoon, is really nothing like "our" sun; it's a bright yellow disk with hairlike rays extending outward, sometimes vibrating rhythmically, like the stars in van Gogh's *Starry Night*. Likewise, there are no shadows, at least not like the shadows of real life. Sometimes, when one of the characters is making a getaway, you can see his shadow following him over the crest of a hill, but the shadow has nothing lifelike about it. It's a big black blob that may, but also may not, obey normal shadow rules: for no reason at all it can suddenly rear up and head off in the opposite direction, or else extend its black arms and hands out to its owner and begin to waltz with him as the background music plays Schubert.

So too, in the spiritual world of cartoons, no one ever dies. Cars go flying off the edge of cliffs, 100-pound weights get dropped from roofs onto the heads of bad guys, the hero himself is flattened into paper-thinness by a steamroller or hit by a series of arrows that go plunk! plunk! plunk!, or else he is catapulted toward a giant tree, around which his elongated body then wraps itself like the coils of a garden hose—no matter, he just dusts himself off and goes on to the next scene. But perhaps most striking is the moral rigidity of the cartoon. Very much like the book of Proverbs, in the cartoon world there are no morally ambiguous figures, at least not in those classic Walt Disney or Hanna-Barbera shorts. Instead, it is always Righteous Mouse against Wicked Cat, and Righteous Mouse will always win out because the righteous are always rewarded. Along with this is the way these cartoons seem out to highlight the treachery of our senses as the proper rewards and punishments are being doled out: what we see in the cartoon is not like normal seeing. And so, pursued by Wicked Cat, Righteous Mouse desperately heads down . . . uh-oh, it's a blind alley! Now he's trapped. But the resourceful rodent whips out a piece of chalk and quickly sketches what looks like the opening of a tunnel on the brick wall in front of him, finishing just in time to hide as Wicked Cat, in hot pursuit, himself turns into the alley. Seeing the tunnel, he naturally heads at it with full force, then cra-a-a-sh! He collapses in a heap as Righteous Mouse emerges from his hiding place and laughs the laugh of the just. But uh-oh! Wicked Cat has picked himself up and is after him again. Now Righteous Mouse heads full speed at the drawing of the tunnel, but—how can this be?—this time it really is a tunnel, and he goes rollicking through it and off into the distance as the befuddled cat scratches his head.

A lot of religious starkness has gone out of public life, but it still finds expression here and there—in gospel music, for example, or in various sorts of devotional literature. Sometimes in the latter, people offer first-person accounts of how they suddenly underwent a conversion experience. Indeed, such accounts are often presented orally now-adays, before microphones in mega-churches or television studios. Some of these experiences (perhaps even a great many) sound as if they were, in some fashion, self-induced—but that is not particularly relevant (or given to investigation) here. Rather, what is interesting is the "rhetoric of starkness" used so consistently in such narratives. Here is that same bright light shooting down into the darkness:

"All at once the glory of God shone upon and round about me in a manner almost marvelous. . . . A light perfectly ineffable shone in my soul, that almost prostrated me on the ground. This light seemed like the brightness of the sun in every direction. It was too intense for the eyes. . . ."

"The very heavens seemed to open and pour down rays of light and glory. Not for a moment only, but all day and night, floods of light and glory seemed to pour through my soul, and oh, how I was changed, and everything became new. My horses and hogs and even everybody seemed changed."

"Looking up, I thought I saw that same light, though it appeared different; and as soon as I saw it, the design was opened to me, according to his promise, and I was obliged to cry out: 'Enough, enough, O blessed God!' The work of conversion, the change, and the manifestations of it are no more disputable than that light which I see, or anything that ever I saw."

"After the choking and stifling had passed away, I seemed at first in a state of utter blankness; then came flashes of intense light, alter-nating with blackness, and with a keen vision of what was going on in the room around me, but no sensation of touch. I thought that I was near death, when, suddenly, my soul became aware of

101

God, who was manifestly dealing with me, handling me, so to speak, in an intense personal present reality. I felt him streaming in like light upon me."

"Realization of conversion was very vivid, like a ton's weight being lifted from my heart; a strange light which seemed to light up the whole room (for it was dark); a conscious supreme bliss which caused me to repeat 'Glory to God' for a long time."

These bits of testimony, collected by the early psychologist and student of religion William James (1842–1910) in his pioneering work *The Varieties of Religious Experience,* all sound oddly similar. Perhaps they are indeed the product of some set of conversion-narrative conventions, or were at least influenced by earlier conversion narratives, going back to that of Saul of Tarsus ("Now as he was going along and approaching Damascus, suddenly a light from heaven flashed around him," Acts 9:3), if not earlier. But the flash of light is not the only "stark" thing about these narratives. They likewise speak of a world altogether changed, in which familiar sights and objects take on a new, elemental look:

"After this my sense of divine things gradually increased and became more and more lively, and had more of that inward sweetness. The appearance of everything was altered; there seemed to be, as it were, a calm, sweet cast, or appearance of divine glory, in almost everything. God's excellency, his wisdom, his purity and love, seemed to appear in everything; in the sun, moon, and stars; in the clouds and blue sky; in the grass, flowers, and trees; in the water and all nature; which used greatly to fix my mind. And scarce anything, among all the works of nature, was so sweet to me as thunder and lightning; formerly nothing had been so terrible to me. Before, I used to be uncommonly terrified with thunder, and to be struck with terror when I saw a thunderstorm rising; but now, on the contrary, it rejoices me."

"It was like entering another world, a new state of existence. Natural objects were glorified, my spiritual vision was so clarified that I saw beauty in every material object in the universe, the woods were vocal with heavenly music; my soul exulted in the love of God, and I wanted everybody to share in my joy."

Certainly not all such experiences are as dramatic as those reported by James's informants. One account that has always struck me by its connection to the starkness I have been describing (despite its altogether understated nature) comes from one of the most coolly reflective writers on religion in antiquity, the first-century Jewish philosopher and biblical interpreter Philo of Alexandria. Philo's hometown of Alexandria, Egypt, was a Greek-speaking city, and he had been educated in the great classics of Greek philosophy as well as in the Hebrew Bible and Judaism. He eventually wrote a multivolume commentary on the Pentateuch (a work that, somewhat paradoxically, ended up having a far greater influence on early Christians than on Jews). At one point in this work, Philo turns his attention to the biblical figure Abraham, who, by his own time (though certainly not in the Hebrew Bible itself), had come to be thought of as the "discoverer" of monotheism, the "first person to declare openly," according to one of Philo's contemporaries, "that there is one God." Philo does more than assert that Abraham was a monotheist; he actually describes how this came about, and although he seems to be talking about Abraham, he was really talking about himself.

The world in which Philo lived—at least according to his own description—was surprisingly modern. Greek mathematicians and scientists were busy studying all the ways of nature and discovering some if its hidden patterns; soon everything, it seemed, would be reduced to formulas and immutable laws. Philo projected this state of affairs back to Chaldea, the place in which Abraham had been born. Here is how he puts it:

The Chaldeans exercised themselves most especially with astronomy and attributed all things to the movements of the stars, believing that whatever is in the world is governed by forces encompassed in numbers and numerical proportions. They exalted the existence of what is visible, and took no thought for what is perceivable to the mind and yet invisible. But seeking out the numerical arrangement according to the cycles of the sun, moon, the planets, and the fixed stars, as well as the changes of the yearly seasons and the overall connection of the things of heaven with what happens on earth, they supposed that the world itself was a god, sacrilegiously making out that which is created to be like the One who had created it.

He [Abraham] grew up with this idea and was a true Chaldean for some time, until, opening the soul's eye from the depth of sleep, he came to behold the pure ray in place of deep darkness, and he followed that light and perceived what he had not seen before, One who guides and steers the world, presiding over it and managing its affairs.

Here, too, is that bright light reported by James's informants, though now it is down to a single ray ("opening the soul's eye from the depth of sleep, he came to behold the pure ray in place of deep darkness"). But equally "stark" is the notion that our eyes and ears aren't telling us the whole story—that the world of the senses is inherently treacherous because it somehow covers over the "real" reality. That is, there exists a certain way of perceiving which is outside of our normal senses, so that the way that world is constantly being described to us may not actually cover everything that is there. Abraham's sudden perception, according to Philo, was not just something new, but something that ran counter to the whole "Chaldean" way of trying to grasp reality; in place of "deep darkness," suddenly there was a light.

✦ ✦ ✦

Some of this sense of starkness can also be glimpsed in the work of one of the greatest philosophers of the twentieth century, Ludwig Wittgenstein (1889–1951). Born in Vienna into a fabulously wealthy (but somewhat quirky) family, Wittgenstein enjoyed a pampered youth. He himself was rather like the computer geeks of our own age—he connected better with machines and ideas than with people. At the age of ten, he managed to build his own model sewing machine out of spare bits of wood and wire. In school, however, he was stiff and formal with his classmates, projecting an aristocratic stuffiness. He went on to study engineering at university, first in Berlin and later at Victoria University in Manchester, where he worked on aeronautical engines. His patent on an improvement in propeller technology dates from 1910.

While in England he became interested in the logical foundations of mathematics and the work of the British logician Bertrand Russell; at length he resolved to study with him. Russell was later to describe his student as "the most perfect example I have ever known of genius as traditionally conceived: passionate, profound, intense, and dominating." Logic is probably the branch of philosophy closest to geekdom, and the book that emerged out of Wittgenstein's studies with Russell, the *Tractatus Logico-Philosophicus,* is an attempt to apply the most rigorous logical standards to the problems philosophy traditionally poses itself. "Perhaps this book will be understood only by someone who has himself already had the thoughts that are expressed in it," Wittgenstein wrote on the opening page, "or at least similar thoughts. So it is not a textbook." In his book, Wittgenstein sought to apply the spare language of mathematical exactitude to an understanding of the world, proposition by proposition. This does not always make for light reading:

2.02331 Either a thing has properties that nothing else has, in which case we can immediately use a description to distinguish it from the others and refer to it; or, on the other hand, there are several things that have the whole set of their properties in common, in which case it is quite impossible to indicate one of them. For if there is nothing to distinguish a thing, I cannot distinguish it, since otherwise it would be distinguished after all.

But an amazing thing happens toward the end of the *Tractatus.* Wittgenstein, who had initially appeared highly suspicious of religion in his search for "just the facts," came to assert that his attempt (or anyone else's) at rigorous description must necessarily fall short of reality:

5.5571 If I cannot say a priori what elementary propositions there are, then the attempt to do so must lead to obvious nonsense.

5.6 The limits of my language mean the limits of my world.

5.61 Logic pervades the world: the limits of the world are [thus] also its limits. So we cannot say in logic, "The world has this in it, and this, but not that." For that would appear to presuppose that we were excluding certain possibilities, and this cannot be the case, since it would require that logic should go beyond the limits of the world; for only in that way could it view those limits from the other side as well. We cannot think what we cannot think; so what we cannot think we cannot say either.

The famous concluding sentence of the *Tractatus,* "Whereof one cannot speak, thereof must one be silent," follows from this. It was misunderstood by some early readers as meaning that philosophical discourse ought to consider only the things that one *can* speak of, because that is all there is to the world. In fact, Wittgenstein's point was quite the opposite. Some philosophical problems are illegitimate because they try to say what cannot be said. As he wrote elsewhere, "To believe in God means to see that the facts of the world are not the end of the matter."

✦ ✦ ✦

Starkness is indeed far removed from the usual "facts of the world" and our normal ways of perceiving. Philo pursued just this point in the continuation of the passage cited above, cleverly connecting Abraham's moment of understanding to the biblical account of his subsequent journey to Canaan. On the way there, according to the Bible, Abraham stopped off in a place call Haran and stayed there for some time before continuing on to the Promised Land. Why this layover? Philo points out that the name "Haran" is similar to the Hebrew word for holes, *horin*. It was necessary, Philo said, for Abraham to go behind the "holes" of the senses, the eyes, ears, and the other orifices through which we normally perceive the outside world; only after going behind them, behind Wittgenstein's "facts of the world," could Abraham be made ready for the final leg of his journey, which would lead to the land of Canaan itself.

I think that is why the night sometimes plays an important part in starkness. When things grow quiet and the world goes dark, people's minds are freed to see and hear what they do not normally perceive:

> For God speaks time and again, though man does not perceive it.
> In a dream, in a night vision, when deep sleep falls on people as
>   they slumber in their beds,
> then it is He opens people's understanding . . . (Job 33:14–16)

> At night I yearn for You with all my being,
> I seek You out with the spirit deep inside me.
> For when Your judgments are [carried out] on earth,
> those who live in the world learn righteousness.
> If the wicked man is pardoned, righteousness is not learned;
> in the land of uprightness, he still does evil.
> He does not perceive God's splendor. (Isaiah 26:9–10)

In the Valley of the Shadow

You have visited me at night, searched my mind . . . (Psalm 17:3)

Throughout the night's watch my eyes stay open. I am awake but
    do not speak.
My thoughts turn to days of old, to years gone by.
Let me say my prayer at night; let me commune with my own
    heart and my spirit will be searching. (Psalm 77:5–7)

On the twenty-fourth day of the eleventh month, the month of
Shebat, in the second year of Darius, the word of the LORD came
to the prophet Zechariah son of Berechiah son of Iddo; and Zechariah said, "In the night I saw a man riding on a red horse! He
was standing among the myrtle trees in the glen; and behind him
were red, sorrel, and white horses. Then I said, 'What are these,
my lord?' The angel who talked with me said to me, 'I will show
you what they are.'" (Zechariah 1:7–9)

While I was shepherding [the flocks] at Abelmaul, the spirit of the
understanding of the Lord came to me, and I saw how all men
were going astray, and how injustice had built walls for itself and
lawlessness was enthroned in towers. And I was grieved for the
race of the sons of men, and I prayed to the Lord to be saved. Then
sleep fell upon me, and I saw a high mountain, and I was on it.
And behold, the skies were opened and an angel of the Lord said
to me: Levi, enter. (*Testament of Levi,* 2:3–6)

I was in the house alone. And I lay on my bed, sleeping. And while
I slept, a great distress entered my heart, and I was weeping with
my eyes in a dream. And I could not figure out what this distress
might be, [nor] what might be happening to me. Then two huge
men appeared to me, the likes of which I had never seen on earth.
Their faces were like the shining sun; their eyes were like burning lamps; from their mouths fire was coming forth; their cloth-
ing had the appearance of froth; their wings were more glistering

108

than gold; their hands were whiter than snow. And they stood at the head of my bed and called me by name. Then I awoke from my sleep, and then I saw those [same] men really standing in front of me. (*2 Enoch* [J version], ch. 1)

Dreams, of course, are the prime real estate of starkness, but what is striking is how—as in the last sentence cited above—the thing dreamed can sometimes cross over into this world: "Then I awoke from my sleep, and then I saw those [same] men really standing in front of me." Were they *really* standing in front of him? I wouldn't be ready to wager on that. But there always have been dreams that strike us as much more than empty swevening; their starkness seems *true* in a way that persists even after we wake up, so that for a time it coexists in our minds alongside all the pastel shades of our ambiguous, workaday existence.

I have always been fond of Jerome's account of a certain dream he had. This fourth-century Christian saint and scholar had a deep love of classical Latin literature; in fact, it was Jerome's mastery of Latin style that led Pope Damasus to commission him to retranslate the Bible (his translation ultimately became the official Vulgate Bible mentioned above). But loving Latin literature carried a price in Jerome's day. The classical authors' espousal of pagan beliefs and their depictions of things that were altogether despicable to Christian readers meant that reading their books and poems was considered sinful. For a time, official doctrine even forbade Christians from serving as teachers in Roman schools, lest by teaching the classics they fall guilty of inculcating false ideas into the minds of their students. And certainly purchasing or possessing books written by the pagan authors was nothing a true Christian ought to do. Yet Jerome had preserved from his youth an extensive (and expensive!) collection of Roman classics, and he was reluctant to part from them. This caused him considerable torment and inner struggle: "And so I, poor fellow, would fast and then read my Cicero; after nights of successive vigils, and after the tears that the recollection of my past sins would wrench from my innermost breast, there, back in my hands again, would be Plautus . . ."

This struggle continued until Jerome at one point fell gravely ill. His fever mounted into the danger zone, he reports, and those attending him began to think he would not make it.

> Arrangements were made for my funeral, and through my chill body the warmth of the breath of life now pulsed only in my luke-warm chest.
>
> Suddenly, I found myself seized up in the spirit and I was handed over to the divine tribunal. There was such light, and so great was the splendor emanating from those standing about, that I, cast down upon the ground, did not dare to look up around me. I was asked what my status was. But when I answered that I was a Christian, the One in charge replied, "You lie. You are a Cicero-nian, not a Christian. For 'where your treasure is, there shall your heart be also' [Matthew 6:21]."
>
> At once I fell silent, and in between blows of the whip—for He had ordered that I be flogged—I was tormented even more by the fires of conscience, and I kept repeating to myself that lit-tle verse, "In the world of the dead, who can confess to Thee?" [Psalm 6:6]. . . . Finally, taking an oath, I called upon His name and said, "O Lord, if ever again I own secular books, if I read them, I will have denied You."

Here, once again, is that blinding light of starkness: "There was such light, and so great was the splendor . . ." But what is particularly striking about Jerome's dream report is the way it carried over into the non–dream world—not just its message ("Stop reading the clas-sics"), but the same insistence seen above that *this was no dream at all:*

> And this was no mere slumbering or an idle dream, such as the ones that often delude us. For I call to witness the tribunal before

which I lay prostrate, and the terrible verdict which caused me to tremble . . . I declare that my shoulders were black and blue, that I felt the bruises long after I awoke from my sleep.

In the winter of 1946–47 there began what has been described as the greatest archaeological find in history: the Dead Sea Scrolls. A group of Bedouin happened upon a cave in the high cliffs that face the Dead Sea south of Jericho. Inside they found some rolled-up manuscripts, written in Hebrew by Jewish scribes more than two millennia earlier. Had the manuscripts not been stored in that particular locale and in the precise way they had been, far from fluctuations in climate or humidity, they would certainly have crumbled into dust long before. But thanks to the unique circumstances of their preservation they survived, and what scholars found when they unrolled them was a major library dating back to biblical times. Some of the books stored there were parts of our Bible, but others seemed to be the writings of the particular group of Jews who put them there, members of an ascetic sect that flourished from the second century BCE until the middle of the first century of the Common Era.

Who were those Jews? Scholars are only now starting to piece together their ideology and way of life, but it is clear that they saw themselves as a community apart. For example, their interpretations of the Bible differed from those of other Jews, but rather than seek to share those interpretations with their coreligionists, they actually had a rule prohibiting the revealing of any of them to anyone who was not a member of their group. They believed that, sooner or later, the "day of revenge" would come, when God would punish everyone except the members of their sect; they would emerge out of the destruction as God's elect. (It didn't turn out that way. There was indeed a great destruction, the Romans' crushing of the Jewish revolt of 68–70 CE, but the members of this religious community were all slaughtered or dispersed and never heard from again.)

The nonbiblical writings that this community left behind are a varied lot. Some of them are lists of rules about how community members are to behave; others are apparently apocalyptic visions of the future; still others are prayers and wise adjurations. Almost all of these have some connection to the starkness I have been discussing, but particularly striking is a collection of some twenty-four "Thanksgiving Hymns," in which the author offers thanks to God for His beneficence. They all begin pretty much the same way:

> I thank You, O Lord, for You have kept me among the living,
>> and have protected me from all the snares of the Pit [i.e.,
>> ruin, destruction].
> For arrogant men have sought [to take] my life, because of my
>> holding fast to Your covenant:
> They are a false lot, an assemblage of Belial [the devil] who do
>> not realize that my standing firm comes from You, and that
>> it is through Your acts of kindness that my life is kept safe,
>> for my steps come from You.

Or again:

> I thank You, Lord, for Your eye keeps watch over my life,
>> saving me from the jealousy of the hypocrites and that band
>> of false interpreters.
> You have redeemed the life of a poor man, whose blood they
>> planned to shed, just because of his serving You.

As these brief excerpts indicate, one striking theme in these hymns is the specific reason given for their expression of gratitude to God. It basically comes down to, "Thanks again for not letting me be killed." Scholars are naturally puzzled by this. Were these hymns the autobiography (real or imagined) of some historical figure—perhaps the founder of this sect? Or are they somehow a picture of the sect's collective identity, persecuted, threatened with death at every turn, but surviving thanks to their heavenly Protector? Whichever the case (and the two alternatives are actually not far apart, since even if they were originally connected to one man, he must have in some sense become an embodiment of the community that sang "his" hymns in their own voice),[3] these compositions are stark from beginning to end. Their world is like that of Edvard Munch, painter of the famous expressionist icon, *The Scream*.

> I thank You, Lord, because You have redeemed me from the
>   Pit, and from Sheol Abadon [the underworld] You have
>   lifted me to eternal heights, so that now I may walk on a
>   boundless plain.
> Surely there is hope for one whom You fashioned from dust to
>   [Your] eternal counsel, and for the twisted spirit whom You
>   purified from great sin, [allowing him] to stand alongside
>   the host of heavenly angels, and come together with the
>   assembly of heavenly beings.
> You have cast the man's fate with the angels of knowledge, to
>   praise Your name in an assembly of joy, and to tell of Your
>   wonders before all of Your creatures.
> But as for me, a thing of clay—what am I? Compounded with
>   water—what can I possibly matter? What power do I
>   have?
> For I have had to stand at the edge of wickedness and share the
>   lot of scoundrels.
> The poor man's soul dwells with great turmoil, and a crushing
>   downfall follows my steps.
> When all the traps of the Pit are open and all the snares of
>   wickedness are spread and scoundrels troll their nets on
>   the water's surface,
> When all the arrows of the Pit fly in every direction and are
>   aimed without consideration,
> When a boundary-line falls on judgment, and anger's lot befalls
>   the forsaken . . .

Has anyone ever been so besieged? Yet this last hymn asserts that God not only saved the speaker's life, but thereupon raised him up to heaven, to join with the angels in praising God. *What could he be talking about?* It's one thing to conceive of yourself as constantly surrounded by the threat of death. But to say in the next breath that you have been exalted to the heights of heaven—joining the angelic choir that, in those days, was conceived to inhabit God's own heavenly temple on high—is to go from one extreme to the other, from the practically dead to God's favorite human being. Yet none of this seems to require any explanation.

All this is oddly reminiscent of John Newton, with whom I began. His self-description ("a wretch like me") sounds very much like the one found here: "the twisted spirit whom You purified from great sin." I suppose one might dismiss this self-understanding, along with the rest of starkness, as some sort of religious delusion, utterly divorced from reality. It certainly is divorced from *ordinary* reality, but that seems to be the whole point: the implicit claim of John Newton, gothic cathedrals, gospel music, Rabbi Akiba, and the Thanksgiving Hymns of the Dead Sea Scrolls is to represent a different reality, more powerful and *truer* than the one we live in every day. It may well be that, after a while, the trappings of starkness became a literary convention, duplicated by artists and artisans who had no firsthand, experiential knowledge of it. But at the beginning, at least, I think the examples I have mentioned and the various snippets I have cited accurately translate a vision of things that is altogether different from our usual one—not exactly otherworldly, but viewing this world with the soul's eye, which reduces (as a modern computer can) the image of a person's face or a mountain landscape to brightly colored blocks of red and yellow and blue, little squares and rectangles that lose the detail in favor of the essence.

8

The Eerie Proximity

The stark world, described in different voices in the previous chapter, is the world of the soul, and there is something both forbidding and inviting about it. People certainly do not enter it as an act of will; in fact, it might be better to say that it enters them. And yet, although it seems to them forbidding, they seem to say that it is *true,* and so, at least after a while, many are drawn back to it—in terms of our own religions, drawn to try to come close to God. This, I suppose, is the real *mysterium tremendum,* since such a yearning never really arises out of any purposeful determination on our part, certainly not out of any hope for personal benefit (though all sorts of religions are fond of claiming to provide such benefits: this will get you salvation; this will give you a good harvest; this will make you better). Thinking about it as arising from something basic in ourselves—arising out of the way all humans used to (and some still do) conceive of themselves, or even out of something built into our brains—may indeed suggest some answers. But whatever and wherever its home base, this reaching out to God—and the eerie proximity of the starkness, its intrusion into everyday reality—simply seem to be a basic part of what it means, or what it has always meant until now, for us to be a religious species.

I didn't know it at the time, but the book I had started writing just before the doctors discovered the cancer dealt with another aspect of this starkness. It began with something I had noticed about angels in the earliest parts of the Hebrew Bible. There are plenty of narratives in the books of Genesis and Exodus and Judges and elsewhere in which someone encounters an angel. The odd thing, however, is that the angel never really *looks* like an angel, that is, he never has the things that angels have in later, Western art—a flowing white robe, large wings protruding from his shoulder blades, and a shiny golden halo suspended over his head. In these biblical stories, the angel always looks just like an ordinary human being, at least at first, so that the person who meets him is quite in the dark. Often, the person carries on an extended conversation with the angel, in which the angel sometimes says the strangest things, but his human interlocutor notices nothing—until suddenly the scales fall from his eyes, and he realizes that this is no ordinary human being at all. Then he usually falls to the ground in reverence, and the angel disappears.

This pattern is repeated in story after story. A brief, almost schematic, example occurs in the book of Joshua, when Joshua encounters the "Angel of the Lord's army":

> And it came to pass, when Joshua was in Jericho, that he lifted up his eyes and saw, and behold! A man was standing across from him with his sword drawn in his hand. So Joshua went up to him and asked, "Are you one of us or one of our enemies?" And he answered, "Neither. But I am the Angel of the LORD's army; I have just arrived." Then Joshua fell face down to the ground in prostration and said to him, "What does my lord wish to say to his servant?" And the Angel of the LORD's army said to Joshua, "Take your shoe from off your foot, for the place upon which you are standing is holy"—and Joshua did so. (Joshua 5:13–15)

Why exactly this little vignette appears in the book of Joshua is not clear, since it stops right there and has no obvious connection either to what precedes or to what follows it. (Some scholars have suggested that the continuation of the narrative has been lost; others have argued that its sole purpose was to suggest a correspondence between Joshua and Moses, since Moses earlier had encountered an angel who demanded precisely the same thing, "Take your shoes from off your feet, for the place upon which you are standing is holy ground"—Exodus 3:5.) In any case, what is striking here is Joshua's inability to recognize this angel as such: at first, at least, he thinks he is seeing just another soldier. This soldier, however, is approaching him with sword unsheathed—certainly an aggressive posture—so Joshua is on his guard, although he is also aware that this may simply be one of his own troops preparing for the battle of Jericho. That is why he asks his nervous question, "Are you on our side or the other side?" When the angel gives his answer, Joshua immediately falls to the ground in obeisance. He is surprised, but not, apparently, utterly flabbergasted: these sorts of things do happen, he seems to be thinking, and now, it is happening to me.

The same sort of thing occurs with Abraham, when three men suddenly show up at his front door:

> The LORD appeared to him [Abraham] at the oak trees of Mamre, as he was sitting near the door of his tent during the hot part of the day. He looked up and saw three men standing near him. As soon as he saw them he ran from the tent door to meet them, and bowed to the ground. "Gentlemen," he said, "if you please, do not, I pray, just pass your servant by. Let a little water be brought so that you can wash your feet and rest underneath this tree. Then I will fetch a bit of bread so that you may satisfy your hunger before resuming your journey—after all, you have come this way to your servant's place." They replied, "Do just as you have said." (Genesis 18:1–5)

The story begins with the assertion that "The LORD appeared to him," but this is said from the narrative's perspective. What Abraham sees are three *men,* whom he receives with characteristic oriental courtesy, providing them with (precious) water to wash their feet and offering them a meal before they continue their journey. He has no idea that they are anything but men; even their gruff response, "Do just as you have said," does not tip him off that something else is afoot.

> Then Abraham hurried into the tent to Sarah and said: "Quick! Knead three *seahs* of choice flour and makes some loaves." Next, Abraham ran to the cattle and chose a calf, nice and tender, which he gave to the servant boy to prepare right away. After that, he took curds and milk, along with the calf that had been prepared, and set them out before them. Then he stood by under a tree while they ate.
>
> They said to him, "Where is your wife Sarah?" and he answered, "In there, inside the tent." Then one said, "I will be back this time next year, and your wife Sarah will have a son." Sarah had been listening at the door of the tent, which was in back of him. Now Abraham and Sarah were old, well advanced in years; Sarah had stopped having the periods that women have. So Sarah laughed to herself, saying, "After I am all used up will I still have relations— not to mention that my husband is old too!" Then the LORD said to Abraham, "Why did Sarah laugh, saying, 'Can I really give birth, old as I am?' Is anything too much for the LORD? I will be back this time next year, and Sarah will have a son." Then Sarah denied it, saying, "I didn't laugh," since she was frightened. But He replied, "Yes you did." (Genesis 18:6–15)

As the passage continues, Abraham is still in a fog. Even their question, "Where is your wife Sarah?"—but how do these strangers know his wife's name?—arouses no curiosity in him. It is only after one of the strangers has announced that Sarah, who had been plagued all these years by infertility, will at last give birth, that the couple begins to understand that these are no ordinary visitors. Then, of course, Sarah is afraid; "I didn't laugh," she says, fearing that her irreverent smirk might bring down divine punishment upon her. (It doesn't, but in commemoration of the incident, the son she bears is given the name "Isaac," which in Hebrew sounds like it comes from the word "laugh.")

A noteworthy feature of this brief narrative is the way that three angels seem to slide effortlessly into being God. After having been treated all along as "men," suddenly their outward appearance fades and the text says: "Then the LORD said to Abraham, 'Why did Sarah laugh . . .'" The usual explanation for this switch in identity is that the angels here are speaking *for* God, so their words are identified as God's own. But this same switch happens again and again in angel stories, too often to be a coincidence; it seems instead to be intended to reflect something basic about the very concept of "angel" in these narratives: it is an altogether transitory state. So whether the text actually calls them angels or "men" (as here), that act of identification matters very little, since it is in any case fleeting, a kind of optical illusion. By the end, the human mask always drops, and it is God who speaks directly to the human beings.

The same sort of thing is evidenced when Moses is first drawn to the burning bush:

> He . . . led the flocks past the wilderness and came to Horeb, the mountain of God. An angel of the LORD appeared to him in a fiery flame from the midst of a bush. He looked, and the bush was burning, but it was not consumed. Moses said: "Let me go and have a look at this amazing sight; why isn't that bush burning up?" When the LORD saw that he had turned aside to look, God called to him out of the bush, "Moses! Moses!" and he said, "Here I am." (Exodus 3:1–4)

Here too, Moses is at first confused; what he sees is identified in the text as an angel, but one who has taken the form of a fiery flame inside a bush. His casual "Let me go and have a look . . ." indicates that he so far suspects nothing supernatural. But then, this fiery flame suddenly dissolves into being God Himself; Moses' initial impression, like Abraham's, turns out to have been an optical illusion.

Jacob's famous wrestling match with an "angel" is yet another such incident:

> And Jacob was left alone, and a man wrestled with him until the break of day. When he saw that he could not overcome him, he wrenched Jacob's hip in its socket, so that the socket of Jacob's hip was strained in the fight with him. Then he said, "Let go of me, since it is getting to be dawn." But Jacob said, "I will not let you go unless you bless me." He said, "What is your name?" and he answered, "Jacob." He said, "Your name will not be Jacob any longer, but Israel, since you have struggled with God and with men and have prevailed. Then Jacob said to him, "Please, now, tell me your name." He answered, "Why should you be asking for my name?" and he blessed him there. Jacob named the place Peniel, saying, "I have seen God face to face and yet my life has been spared." (Genesis 32:25–31)

Here, Jacob actually *wrestles* with this apparition (called a "man" here and not an angel)[1] and even suffers physical harm at his hands—his hip is thrown out of joint. There can be little doubt in his mind that this is a flesh-and-blood adversary. True, after his apparent victory, Jacob asks his opponent to bless him, but this does not mean he has figured out that his wrestling partner is divine; it's more like "Say 'Uncle'" in our own hand-to-hand combat. What is more, his follow-up request, "Please, now, tell me your name," indicates that he still hasn't figured things out, since this is nothing you would say to an angel: it was a well-known fact in those days that angels didn't have names.[2] It is only the angel's reply that tips Jacob off to what was happening—and then, interestingly enough, he does not say, "I have seen *an angel of* God face to face"; it is God Himself that he has been (as it were) wrestling with all along.

The spiritual world of classical Greece and Rome was far from that of ancient Israel, even if, in chronological and geographic terms, they were not that distant. Here gods sometimes beget humans or turn themselves into humans, or else they turn humans into trees or animals or all sorts of other things. Yet it is striking that in Greek and Latin literature one sometimes finds narratives rather similar to the biblical examples just seen. In Homer's *Iliad,* for example, gods and goddesses frequently come down to earth disguised as ordinary humans and intervene in their affairs. Thus, swift-footed Iris, goddess of the rainbow, pretends to be Polites, son of the Trojan king Priam, or dresses up like Laodice, Priam's daughter. Sometimes such deceptions are spotted right away, but at other times it takes a while:

> Then the goddess [Aphrodite] spoke to her [Helen] in the likeness of an old woman, a wool-comber who used to card wool for her when she lived in Lacedaemon . . . "Come here!" [she said]. "Alexander [i.e., Helen's seducer, Paris] is calling you home. He's in his room on his inlaid bed, gleaming in his beautiful attire. You wouldn't think that he had just finished fighting an enemy! Rather, he looks as if he were going to a dance, or rather, as if he had just finished dancing and sat down."
>
> So she spoke, and stirred Helen's heart in her breast. But when she [Helen] caught a glimpse of the goddess's beautiful neck, of her lovely breast and her flashing eyes, she was shocked. Then she spoke to her, saying: "Strange goddess, why are you determined to fool me like this . . ."

At first Helen is taken in, just as in the biblical passages cited: Helen's heart is sincerely stirred. But Aphrodite's disguise isn't perfect: her godlike neck, her breast, and flashing eyes give her away, and Helen catches on.

Here is an extended example of the same phenomenon, this time from Virgil's *Aeneid.* Venus, the divine mother of the human Aeneas, appears to her son after he and his men have been shipwrecked on the shores of Libya:

His mother appeared to him standing along the way in the midst of the forest. She had a girl's face and clothes, and even carried the weapons of a girl from Sparta . . . Like a hunter, she had a bow hanging handily from her shoulder, and she let her hair blow loose in the wind. The top part of her garment was gathered with a knot, leaving her knees bare. "Hey, you fellows," she called [to Aeneas and his companions], "have you by any chance seen a sister of mine wandering near here?" . . . Then the son of Venus [Aeneas] began his reply: "I have not heard or seen anything of your sisters—Say, what should I be calling you, young maiden? For you really don't have the face of a mortal, nor does your voice sound human . . . Certainly you're a goddess then—a sister of Apollo? Or maybe some sort of nymph? Anyway, whoever you are, please be kind and give us a hand—tell us what skies we are under now, and on which of the world's shores we have been cast . . ."

Just as in the biblical examples, here too the deity's appearance seems at first altogether human: Venus is disguised as a young maiden out for a day of hunting in the forest. Aeneas is taken in entirely; in fact, contemplating her beautiful face and shapely legs, he comes out with what must be the oldest and tiredest come-on line invented by man: "Say, honey, what's your name?" But at that very minute he suddenly senses something is up: she must be some kind of goddess, or at least a nymph. It is certainly remarkable that this realization doesn't seem to faze him in the slightest. Apparently, everyday life simply *can* involve encounters with gods or goddesses sometimes.

Venus of course keeps up the deception, denying that she is a goddess: "I'm just a Tyrian girl," she tells him, and then goes on to answer Aeneas's questions in a passage that stretches over the next seventy lines or so. All the while her son keeps looking and listening attentively, never suspecting that this is his own divine mother. But then, at the end, there is something about her neck that gives her away:

She spoke, but as she turned away, a glint of rose shone forth from her neck, and her heavenly hair exhaled its godly perfume. Her garment now flowed down to her very feet, and by her demeanor she was revealed to be a true goddess. Now he recognized his mother and pursued her with these words as she vanished: "Why do you cruelly delude your own son with disguises? Why not have our hands clasp each other and have our voices speak and reply in truth?" With such words he reproved her, then headed off toward the walls of the city. (*Aeneid* 1:314–37; 402–10)

No doubt such encounters were simply a literary convention by the time of Virgil, who lived in the first century BCE. Perhaps even in Homer's time, eight centuries earlier, they had already become conventional. But their existence, indeed, their uncanny resemblance to the biblical passages seen, suggests that the convention in both places must ultimately go back to what once seemed a normal depiction of reality. Such divine-human encounters simply did occur, and when they did, the people involved at first did not understand what was going on. Whatever it was that they thought they were perceiving, they at first processed that perception with the everyday tools we usually use for such processing, our eyes and ears. (In a sense, this might be compared to dreaming: when we report on a dream, we say, "I saw a man in a blue suit take out a pearl-handled revolver; then I heard this enormous bang . . ." But of course we actually *saw* and *heard* nothing at all; it's just that our brain processed the dream as if we had. In fact, sleep researchers report that, during a dream, our eyes dart about behind our closed eyelids as if they were indeed seeing something.) But then, after a while, the fog lifts and the person understands that this is no ordinary human being at all.

The thing that struck me as so interesting about these examples is what they seemed to say not only about the "other world," but consequently about *this* world for people at that time. Long, long ago, everyday life must have had a different quality, a different tone, from that of our lives today: it was *ominous* in a way that ours is not. At one point or another, it seems, anyone might encounter a stranger who, after a while, would turn out to be an angel/God/a god. I don't believe, of course, that this was the everyday experience of ancient Israelites or ancient Greeks—I'm quite sure that most went through their lives without such encounters. But what these narratives are saying is that such things really *can* and do happen, indeed, they happened in the past to well-known people—and these very assertions must have sometimes made people think twice, not only about the unusual stranger they met at the market this morning, but about all of reality. The starkness was always just over there, concealing itself behind the drab colors of the everyday.

Thinking about this, I came back to what the anthropologist E. E. Evans-Pritchard had written about the Azande, a people of central Africa whom he had studied in the 1920s.* He was particularly interested in the role of *mangu* (roughly: "witchcraft") in their daily life:

> I had no difficulty in discovering what Azande think about witchcraft, nor in observing what they do to combat it. These ideas and actions are on the surface of their life and are accessible to anyone who lives for a few weeks in their homesteads. Every Zande is an authority on witchcraft. There is no need to consult specialists. There is not even need to question the Azande about it, for information flows freely from recurrent situations in their social life, and one has only to watch and listen . . .
>
> Witchcraft is ubiquitous. It plays a part in every activity of Zande life; in agriculture, fishing, and hunting pursuits; in domestic life of homesteads as well as in communal life of district and court; it is an important theme of mental life, in which it forms the

---

* "E-P," as Evans-Pritchard was known, taught social anthropology at Oxford, where he was the teacher of (among others) Godfrey Lienhardt, whose study of the Dinka was cited earlier.

background of a vast panorama of oracles and magic; its influence
is plainly stamped on law and morals, etiquette and religion; it is
prominent in technology and language; there is no niche or corner
of Zande culture into which it does not twist itself. If blight seizes
the ground-nut crop it is witchcraft; if the bush is scoured in vain
for game it is witchcraft; if women laboriously bale water out of
a pool and are rewarded by but a few small fish it is witchcraft; if
termites do not rise when their swarming is due and a cold, useless night is spent in waiting for their flight it is witchcraft; if a
wife is sulky and unresponsive to her husband it is witchcraft; if
a prince is cold and distant with his subjects it is witchcraft; if a
magical rite fails to achieve its purpose it is witchcraft; if, in fact,
any failure or misfortune falls upon anyone at any time and in
relation to any of the manifold activities of his life it may be due
to witchcraft . . .

To us witchcraft is something which haunted and disgusted our
credulous ancestors. But the Zande expects to come across witchcraft at any time of day or night. He would be just as surprised
if he were not brought into daily contact with it as we would be
if confronted by its appearance. To him there is nothing miraculous about it. It is expected that a man's hunting will be injured by
witches, and he has at his disposal means of dealing with them.
When misfortunes occur he does not become awestruck at the
play of supernatural forces. He is not terrified at the presence of
an occult enemy. He is, on the other hand, extremely annoyed.[3]

I suppose one could substitute "God" for "witchcraft" in the above
passage and, with the possible exception of the very last sentence,
have an altogether orthodox Christian or Jewish or Muslim understanding of the world. It's not, of course, that the Azande don't attribute anything *positive* to the supernatural—they have their own
divine providers of beneficence, who represent the good side of our
single deity. But witchcraft is symptomatic of their ongoing interaction with all that is part of the "other world" (except that, for them,

that "other world" interferes so regularly with their own that they would rightly object to calling it "other").[4]

In mentioning these things, I may seem to have gone over to the side of religion's pooh-poohers. After all, everyone today knows what can bring about an unsuccessful hunt or the failure of a groundnut crop, and it has nothing to do with witchcraft. But I think that simply to dismiss Azande *mangu,* to shrug it off as part of a superstitious primitivism from which we have happily been weaned, is to miss something essential. The world inhabited by the Azande, indeed, by our pre-Homeric, prebiblical ancestors, was first and foremost one in which *we* were different, and our being different made everything else different too. Back then, we fit snugly into our place in a world that was overwhelmed by divinity, and even if the forms in which the divine presented itself to us—the successful hunt or harvest, the encounter with a mysterious stranger—were necessarily drawn from the world of our own experience (a bit like the sights and sounds of a dream), such was simply the way in which this great, underlying divine presence made itself known to us.

This is not an insignificant matter, and it ultimately leads back to the state of mind with which I began these reflections. Of course, that sense of the music stopped, and of being contained within one's borders, is definitely different from the state of mind of the Zande farmer discoursing on magic. But what they have in common is the space they leave open, and how that space is filled—with our yearning for, or fear of, or simply our raw awareness of, the divine. This reality, the reality not screened out, is never far, in fact, it is just over there, no matter in what form it presents itself. Oddly enough, however, one thing that helped to put its eerie proximity almost out of reach was Israel's great contribution to human thought, monotheism.

Scholars have been aware for a long time of a certain "disconnect" between the version of God preached by Judaism and Christianity—an all-knowing, omnipresent, and all-powerful deity—and the way in which God is depicted in, especially, some of the earliest parts of the Hebrew Bible. There, He is not omnipresent: much of the time He is up in heaven, and He "goes down" from there to destroy the Tower of Babel (Genesis 11:7) or to check up on the people of Sodom (18:21) or to speak with Moses (Exodus 34:5); indeed, He "walks about" in the Garden of Eden (Genesis 3:8). Going from one place to another or walking about are not things you do if you are omnipresent. Nor, actually, is He ever said to be omniscient: indeed, when Adam and Eve hide themselves in the bushes, He calls out, "Where are you?" and after Cain kills his brother and hides the body, He asks, "Where is your brother, Abel?" He tests Abraham's faithfulness by ordering him to sacrifice his son Isaac—but why should an all-knowing deity need to put Abraham and Isaac through such an ordeal if He knows in any case how it will turn out? And why, at the end, does He tell Abraham, "Now I know that you are one who fears God"? *Now I know* means I didn't know before. Examples could be multiplied.

For some time, scholars and clergymen and just ordinary Bible readers have had the same answer when this "disconnect" is pointed out: in those days, they say, people could not understand complicated ideas like omniscience and omnipresence. But this seems most unlikely. It is very easy to say in biblical Hebrew, "God is everywhere," and, "God knows everything," so there was certainly no linguistic barrier, and if you say such things in English nowadays to a five- or six-year-old, the child will have no difficulty understanding what you mean. How complicated could it have been three thousand years ago?

The real answer is that these most ancient biblical stories present a different "model" of God (I mean "model" here the way modern physicists use the word, as a way of depicting that which is not perceivable by the eye or ear). This model was not the omnipresent, omniscient model we have nowadays, but in its own way, it was no less sophisticated. In this understanding of things, God is not everywhere, but just on the other side of the curtain that separates ordinary reality from the extraordinary; there He stays most of the time, in eerie proximity, but every once in a while He crosses over. When this happens, human beings are at first confused; they are in a fog, like Joshua or Abraham or Jacob. But then, after a while, the truth dawns on them. When this happens they may be surprised, but they are not flabbergasted; everyone knows about the eerie proximity.

What is striking about this model is its focus on human *perception*. Reality seems to be one thing, but then it turns out to be something else entirely (just as it does for Righteous Mouse and Wicked Cat). If the only thing that these biblical narratives wished to communicate was that God appeared to Joshua or Abraham or Jacob, then the text needed to say no more than that, indeed, the angel who appears in them might well have been decked out in such a way as to be immediately recognizable. But perception was the whole point of this model. People had to be in a fog at first. Only after something clicked inside their heads could the stark truth begin to dawn on them.

Since this is not the "omnipresent" model in any case, there really was no problem in depicting God in human form—this physical manifestation would in any case be revealed to be illusory. So God is regularly presented as humanlike: He "stands" next to Moses on Mount Sinai and "passes in front of him" (Exodus 34:5–6); from the context it would appear that, in this visionary moment, God is not much bigger in size than Moses. Elsewhere, He speaks with Moses "mouth to mouth" (Numbers 12:8). Of course, Moses is altogether exceptional. Most people never "see" God; He is usually on the other side of the curtain, and even when He does cross over, He is often surrounded by a shielding cloud (Exodus 34:5), since "no one can see Me and live" (Exodus 33:20).

How does one get from this sort of a God—whose human form appears and disappears again—to the more abstract God of later Judaism, Christianity, and Islam, the one who is always there, the omnipresent and omniscient Supreme Being? Scholars have pointed to various things—a greater, more universal perspective that unfolded in the wake of the Babylonian conquest of Jerusalem in 586 BCE and the subsequent exile of much of the population for the next half century (being forced to live in another country brought with it the need for a broader, indeed, universal, perspective). Perhaps even before that, the influence of Assyrian royal ideology on Jewish thinking, or the universality characteristic of Mesopotamian and Egyptian wisdom literature, also played a role. But along with these one must consider the very rise of monotheism, which in turn generated a new attitude toward starkness, and our desire somehow to keep the supernatural at arm's length. On this, more presently.

9

The Sickening Question

And so, along with the music-stopped smallness comes the starkness, eerily close. The starkness that I saw in those biblical stories is there as well in the other things I have discussed—the medieval paintings and cathedral architecture and the Dead Sea Scrolls and gospel album covers and Philo of Alexandria and "Amazing Grace." But I noticed it in one more thing worth mentioning, something that, not coincidentally, people who are gravely ill will recognize at once.

The sickening question may not occur to you right away, but at some point it does, as it does to everyone who has reason to believe he's not going to be here in six months, or even two years or three. You look around at your elderly colleagues, or just at old people in the subway, people on the street, that white-haired gent, for example, coming toward you on slow but steady legs, carrying a heavy plastic bag labeled "Kay Bee Toys" (for his grandchildren, no doubt). It's a really stupid question, the kind about which Ecclesiastes said, "You're not asking about that out of wisdom." True indeed; so you put it aside. Still, you have to wonder about it, or, after a while, at least wonder about wondering about it. Why *do* we expect the world to be a fair place? Unfairness is everywhere. "It happens," said the same Ecclesiastes, "that a righteous man perishes in his righteousness, while a wicked man keeps on living in his wickedness." *It happens?* It happens every day! In fact, your own little tragedy is inscribed next to so many big ones on the front page of every newspaper (teen-age soldier cut down for trying to keep the peace; pilgrims blown to smithereens by a suicide bomber) that in no time at all it is just one more instance in an endless litany of unfairnesses—why should anyone ever expect life to be any different? And yet, somehow, we always do; here indeed is something worth wondering about.

At first, the wondering is very low-key. You look at what's actu-ally happening to you right now, and it seems just . . . puzzling. How odd that it should end this way! How especially odd to see those old guys and know that you were never meant to be one of them. "What made us dream that he could comb gray hair?" Yeats asked about a friend's dead son. The only thing that eventually turns this impres-sion of oddness into something worse, into something sickening, is, I suppose, its paradigmatic quality, that is, what it seems to be say-ing *in general* about life's unfairness. It's like some bad smell that you always knew existed, knew that it was back there somewhere, but now you can actually smell it, in fact, the smell is unavoidable, and it speaks of filth and miasma and human detritus. This is what life is *really* like and always was, though you chose not to notice: the smell of life untreated and undisguised.

The finality also has a lot to do with it. We are used to being patient and waiting things out; "You never know." But now that des-tiny is down to its last few inches and it's clear that what *might* be is what actually *will* be, then this merely odd reversal of your normal expectations takes on a different quality. From here you can see the last word in the sentence, the period that is rolled up against its last letter, and it's not a good sentence, it's not what it should have been. *But what right did you have to expect it to be good?* Certainly personal experience and famous biographies and the great sweep of history all teach the opposite. And yet somehow our deepest expectation (so deep it was never formulated in words) is that things are *ultimately* destined to be fair, to be just—except that now "ultimately" is in plain sight and it's not . . . What ever made us think it would be?

This question is often connected to the rise of monotheism in ancient Israel. So long as reality was thought to be the product of different gods—so this argument goes—or even just two (as in the religious dualism of ancient Persia),[1] then there could be no "problem of evil"* in the world. Even an infant death rate that, in ancient times, could be close to 50 percent, even devastating floods such as those that inspired the Mesopotamian *Gilgamesh* epic, as well as seemingly endless famines, outbreaks of deadly plagues, and an earthquake now and then—all these came with their own, ready-made explanation: some gods are good and some are bad (or perhaps many are not particularly either; they just do what they do without giving much thought to the human consequences). And even if there are only two gods, then those two can be thought to be locked in an unending struggle between good and ill. Reality, with all of its ups and downs, is thus easily accounted for, at least in theory, so long as you are not a monotheist.

So it was in the ancient Near East. There was a storm god (in the northwest Semitic orbit he was known as Baal or Hadad), an impetuous, sometimes bellicose deity who wielded his weapons of thunder and lightning. When a storm hit the northern mountains, who was the unseen rider of those clouds if not Baal? What he brought might sometimes cause the rivers to overflow their banks and flood a village or wash out a mountain terrace, but his ministrations also brought good, the life-giving rains, to the eastern Mediterranean. So was he good or bad? One might conclude that he was really neither, as indeed the wind and the rain that he controlled are neither. Elsewhere, in ancient Greece and Rome, the storm winds belonged to Aeolus, a god who was charged with the entire storehouse of winds,

---

* This is the name theologians conventionally give to the contradiction between an all-powerful and beneficent God who nevertheless creates or allows evil to exist in the world. The phrase confuses many English speakers, since it uses the same word, "evil," to refer both to natural catastrophes and to humanly generated evil, *moral* evil. While the Latin *malum* covered both phenomena equally, its common English translation, "evil," elsewhere is generally used to refer to the things that humans undertake to do against one another; the natural catastrophes that afflict us should probably be called by some other name, something like "adversity" or "misfortune."

either gentle zephyrs that help the mariner to his destination, or the huge, crashing storms that shipwrecked Aeneas and his men on the Libyan shore. Both gods were, in this sense, ethically neutral.

If so, it might seem that there is really nothing *theological* at stake for a polytheist in the eruption of natural disaster. The gods are no more consistently good or bad than the phenomena that they control; they may even do bad while intending to do good (since they are not infallible). More to the point, however, is the fact that the gods do not act in isolation; they *interact*. There are other gods who provoke them or restrain them; reality is a product of their interaction. Thus, family spats among the gods often have meteorological consequences. So, as people contemplate reality, they make up stories about the gods—little theories, really, about how these hidden causers might have been relating to one another and so have brought about this or that event on earth that the humans have just witnessed. These are the polytheist's myths. Since reality has a way of repeating—the phases of the moon or the tides, the changing seasons, the cycles of boom or bust, birth and death—the same stories keep playing themselves out, time and again. The Egyptologist Henri Frankfort described the phenomenon clearly:

> The ancients told myths instead of presenting an analysis or conclusions. We would explain, for instance, that certain atmospheric changes broke a drought and brought about rain. The Babylonians observed the same facts but experienced them as the intervention of the gigantic bird Imdugud which came to their rescue. It covered the sky with the black storm clouds of its wings and devoured the Bull of Heaven, whose hot breath had scorched the crops.
>
> In telling such a myth, the ancients did not intend to provide entertainment. Neither did they seek, in a detached way and without ulterior motives, for an intelligible explanation of the natural phenomena. They were recounting events in which they were involved to the extent of their very existence. They experienced

directly a conflict of powers, one hostile to the harvest, the other frightening but beneficial: the thunderstorm reprieved them in the nick of time by defeating and utterly destroying the drought. The images had already become traditional at the time when we meet them in art and literature, but originally they must have been seen in the revelation which the experience entailed.[2]

In a polytheistic world, the vicissitudes of daily life are the end product of conflicts that take place "up there," between competing gods; these conflicts (and other godly interactions) come to be celebrated and ritualized in ancient myths. Understanding the world in the polytheist's way would thus seem to have been relatively easy, at least theoretically. While it certainly hurt him no less to see natural disaster strike, or to see himself or his family stricken, at least adversity did not bring with it that sickening question of the monotheist: "Where is the fairness, the *order,* in all this? How can You, the sole divine power in the world, be making this happen?"

All this is nice in theory, but the theory ought not to be overstated—because in truth, the gods were never really the equivalent of impersonal forces. Rather, they were those great, altogether *personal* powers up there that created reality down here, and at least some of them were invariably identified with our city, our tribe, our empire. They protected us. In doing this, the divine protectors were rarely unopposed; other deities often got in the way. That being the case, it was only natural for us curious humans to speculate about what was going on up there—to try to understand, as Frankfort says, what combination of opposing wills caused things to keep being the way they are. (If your divine protector failed to respond, it might also be that he/she was busy with someone or something else. Patience was required—or sometimes, a nudge from another deity aware of your plight.) But the gods, even though they could theoretically be neutral forces, really never were. This is certainly interesting. Indeed, despite the unfairness of this world, the gods of Mesopotamia, at least, were often identified with the interests of justice and fairness. Thus the Babylonian king Hammurabi, in the preface to the famous law code issued in his name, specifically states that:

> When the august god Anu, king of the Anunnaku deities, and the god Enlil, lord of heaven and earth, who determines the destinies of the land, allotted supreme power over all peoples to the god Marduk, the firstborn son of the god Era, exalting him among the Igigu deities, [they] named the city of Babylon with its august name and made it supreme within the regions of the world and established for him within it eternal kingship, whose foundations are as fixed as heaven and earth.
>
> At that time, the gods Anu and Enlil, for the enhancement of the well-being of the people, named me by my name Hammurabi, the pious prince, who venerates the gods, *to make justice prevail* in the land, to abolish the wicked and the evil, to prevent the strong from oppressing the weak, to rise like the sun-god Shamash [himself associated with dispensing justice] over all humankind to illuminate the land.[3]

As this text makes clear, it was the earthly king's duty to promulgate fair laws and see that justice was done. But the king's mandate to do so came from the gods, as a matter of fact from "Anu, king of the Anunnaku deities, and the god Enlil, lord of heaven and earth," who appointed justice-loving Marduk as supreme god of Babylon; in this as in other ways, these gods are represented as champions of justice and right. Indeed, it was the gods who were responsible for, and identified with, the cosmic order, called *ma'at* in ancient Egypt and *mīsharum* in Mesopotamia: both words sometimes had the narrower meaning of "justice." People apparently assumed that it was simply in the higher powers' nature to be on the side of justice.

There are some reflections of this basic, premonotheistic assumption in the Hebrew Bible. One of them is the expression usually translated as "the fear of God." It may not seem like it, but this expression is altogether different from a similar-sounding one, "the fear of the LORD." The latter actually has nothing to do with what we call "fear": it might best be translated as "the practice of Israel's religion" or "the proper worship of Israel's God." As such, it is something specific to the people of Israel and, as well, something that must be *learned.* "Come, children, listen to me and I will teach you the fear of the LORD" (Psalm 34:12). When the Assyrians resettled northern Israel with foreigners who knew nothing of the local religion, the Assyrians dispatched an Israelite priest, "and he taught them how to fear the LORD" (2 Kings 17:28). Israelites themselves are frequently urged to "*learn* to fear the LORD" (Deuteronomy 14:23, 31:12, etc.).

By contrast, there is nothing Israelite about "the fear of God," and it is not something that is specifically taught. Indeed, because of a well-known ambiguity in biblical Hebrew (whereby the word "God" itself is plural in form and therefore indistinguishable on its own from "the gods"), this expression might often be understood better as "fear of the gods." Thus, when the Israelite Joseph, pretending to be an Egyptian, tells his brothers that he wishes to treat them fairly, his words of reassurance ought not to be translated (as they inevitably are) as "I fear God" (Genesis 42:18). He isn't trying to tell them that he has suddenly become a monotheist or their coreligionist! What he really says is, "I fear the gods," so I'm going to give you a break. Similarly, Abraham, sojourning in the land of Gerar, says to the pagan king Abimelech *not,* "I said to myself that there is no fear of God in this place"—the people of Gerar are certainly neither Israelites nor monotheists—but, "I said to myself that there is no fear of *the gods* in this place" (Genesis 20:11), that is, this is the Wild West, and I really didn't know if your people wouldn't just come up to me and kill me. From both these examples it should further be clear what "fearing the gods" really means: respecting fairness and common decency. This ancient phrase preserved this same coloring even within a monotheistic context: Israelites were ordered to show deference to the elderly, not to exploit one another, not to loan out money at interest, and not to treat slaves ruthlessly (Leviticus 19:32; 25:17, 36, 43), in conjunction with the general commandment to "fear God/ the gods," that is, to have a basic respect for fairness and common decency. But this is precisely my point: this ancient expression highlights the fact that "the gods" in the ancient Near East were just assumed to stand up for justice and right. Anyone who *feared the gods* therefore knew that he had to treat his fellow man fairly—showing deference to the elderly, not taking advantage of the weak, the poor, or the slave—or else the gods, since they were axiomatically associated with fairness, might go after him for not doing so.

Another bit of evidence comes from one of the canonical psalms, one which provides a rare biblical explanation for the world's transition from polytheism to monotheism:

> God stands in the divine assembly, among the gods He passes
>   judgment:
> "How long will you [gods] judge falsely, showing favor to the
>   guilty party?
> Give justice to the poor, the orphan; find in favor of the needy,
>   the wretched.
> Save the poor and the lowly; rescue them from the wicked!"
> But they did not realize or understand, walking about in
>   darkness; the earth's foundations tottered. [So then God
>   told them:]
> "I used to think that you all were gods and sons of the Most
>   High;
> yet you will die like humans, and fall like one of the falling
>   stars."
> Arise, O God, judge the earth, since all the nations now are
>   Yours. (Psalm 82)

This visionary psalm recounts the day when God fired all the other gods. The scene takes place in the "divine assembly" or "council of the gods." That was where, according to a widespread ancient

Near Eastern conceit, the gods would regularly assemble to consider various courses of action; it functioned something like a modern government's cabinet. In Psalm 82, it is the God of Israel who presides over the council, just as the god Anu presided over a similar assembly in Mesopotamia and the god El held court in the mythology of ancient Ugarit. Normally, the council would deliberate and, when a course of action was determined, one or more of its members would be dispatched to carry it out. But in Psalm 82, God has apparently convened the other gods in order to decree their deaths. "I used to think that you all were gods and sons of the Most High," He tells them; as such, of course, they would presumably live forever. But they have failed to do their duty and have thus lost their right to control men's fate, so "you will die like humans, and fall like one of the falling stars." (The phenomenon of shooting stars [really not stars but meteors] was, of course, well known to the ancients; to them it was sometimes construed as the death of a heavenly deity.) Before their downfall, different gods in the divine assembly were associated with specific cities or nations and were presumed to look out for the human residents of their fiefdoms. But once the other gods have been fired and turned into mere mortals, God alone will preside in heaven and look after the fate of *all* peoples: "all the nations now are Yours."

That is the basic sequence of events narrated by this psalm, but what is particularly interesting here is the reason given for the gods' being fired and turned into mortals: they have failed to uphold the interests of justice and fairness. They showed favor to the guilty oppressor instead of dispensing true justice to those whose lives depend on it, the indigent and the wretched, the orphan and all the other powerless people in society. As a result of their failure to perform this most basic duty, the very order of the cosmos was threatened: "the earth's foundations tottered." This dereliction of duty was so grave as to make them unfit to continue as gods, *for what good does it do to have gods if they don't uphold basic justice and fairness?* Thus, even if this particular psalm suggests that at some point the gods fell down on the job, its underlying assumption is the same one we have been tracing, that even in a polytheistic world, where reality can be explained as the imperfect result of different, often competing, powers in heaven, dispensing justice is nevertheless understood to be the gods' common obligation and goal.

But why? With so much evident injustice and unfairness in the world, would it not make more sense to think just the opposite, that the gods care not a whit about such things? This is really the same question as that asked about Boethius earlier: how can someone who has been unfairly condemned to be bludgeoned to death at the age of 45, someone whose whole crime was accepting a high government post and who was thus unexpectedly thrown into the company of white-collar thieves and brigands bent on squashing anyone who stood in their way—how can such a person in his last words assert that the God responsible for all this, the God who controls the whole world, is a fair judge? I am not sure if anyone has ever surveyed all the world's religions in order to see just how widespread this rather counterintuitive presumption of divine justice is. My hunch, in any case, is that it is not by any means limited to the ancient Near East and the religions that grew out of it.

So here is something else glimpsed in the starkness. Whatever the world may ordinarily seem to be, ultimately it is not neutral, not simply a variegated affair of yes-and-no and slight nuances. In order to see things in this way, I think a person has to be (like that spring-loaded tape measure mentioned earlier) sucked back from all over the world into himself, in order to fit into his own, human smallness. It is easy now for religion's deniers to dismiss the way of seeing associated with ancient religions as a benighted patchwork of superstitions and wishful thinking, one that is now happily being disproved and scientifically explained. But my own belief—and the continued theme of this book—is that people two thousand or five thousand years ago were not any stupider than we are today, and that they certainly knew when their own innocent children were dying, whether from disease or famine or apparently nothing at all. So if they maintained that the gods and the cosmic order that they created were fundamentally just, it was not, I think, that they had a different notion of justice, but that they had a different way of fitting into the world, and a different, *stark* way of seeing it up close.

These two—starkness and the musicless, small state of mind with which I began—certainly go together. Because it is that state of mind that makes the starkness accessible in the first place: being drawn back into smallness allows a window to open onto the stark world. In that place of darkness and great light, of absolutes and essences that are far removed from the stippled, reddish, purplish hurts of this existence, divine justice shines through. That is, I suppose, where Moses was when God told him that, despite all the vicissitudes of life, He was by nature "a merciful and compassionate God, abounding in kindness and faithfulness."

It hardly needs to be said that the Bible is not a monochromatic document; what Moses saw was not the only view expressed. After all, we humans still have to live in a world that hurts; however much our own experience or—more often the case—the religious dogma handed down to us from others urges us to accept divine justice despite appearances, the sickening question never quite goes away. The drama of its refusal to be silenced is played out in another part of the Bible, the book of Job, and despite its great antiquity (when Job was written is still the subject of much debate, but it probably should be dated no later than the sixth or fifth century BCE), it still speaks clearly to us moderns.

The story is simple: Job gets wiped out. In one blow he loses everything—his fortune, his children (struck dead by a great windstorm), and shortly thereafter, even his health (his body is covered with "loathsome sores" from head to toe). How could God let this happen? Before all this occurred, Job had been an exemplary devotee of God. In fact, that is what got him into trouble. He was so exemplary that, seeing him, Satan decided to challenge God to a test: "Let me afflict Job as best I can, and then let's see if he remains devoted to You." In other words, let's see what it takes to get him to ask the sickening question.

The author of the book deliberately chose to make Job a non-Israelite. He wanted to depict Job as one of those sages who lived to the south and east of biblical Israel, since they were famous for a doctrine—it might be more proper to say that it was a whole way of viewing the world, a Weltanschauung—that was called, somewhat misleadingly, "wisdom." According to the canons of "wisdom," all of reality obeys a great divine plan devised long ago by the gods, or God. This divine plan includes not only the immutable phenomena of nature—the sun always rises in the east, spring always follows the winter—but as well God's equally immutable ways with humanity. Prominent among wisdom's teachings is the principle of divine reward and punishment: God is an unbiased judge, rewarding the righteous and punishing the wicked. As a north Arabian sage, Job had spent his life espousing this idea, but now it, as much as Job himself, was going to be put to the test. Would he still be able to uphold this basic teaching of wisdom when he himself was suffering so unjustly? Another author might have made Job a stoical hero, but for the writer of this biblical book, the whole point was to have Job fail the test miserably.

True, he starts out toeing wisdom's party line. When—after their children have been killed and their own lives ruined—Job's wife tells him to give up his cherished beliefs because they are obviously wrong, he answers: "You're talking like one of those fools! Should we accept only good things from God and not accept the bad?" But as the deadweight of all that has happened to him starts to sink in, Job's mood turns somber: "Why couldn't I have just died at birth?" he asks. That would have saved everyone a lot of pain.

At this point his "comforters" show up. They are called that because they perform a certain ancient Near Eastern ritual of mourning. When someone had suffered a loss, people in those days would arrive at the sufferer's house and try to get him or her to accept what had happened. At first the sufferer had to "refuse to be comforted" (Genesis 37:35); to do any less would be to trivialize the loss. So the comforters would keep coming back and telling the sufferer things like, "Everyone has to die, and your father really was in a lot of pain—it's better like this," or, "Yes, I know it's terrible, but, you know, there's a lot of suffering in the world besides what's happened to you . . . ," and similar things, until finally the sufferer accepted his loss, that is, accepted "to be comforted." In Job's case, the comforters are not family members but people who, like Job himself, are expert in the doctrines of wisdom; their foreign names and windy rhetoric suggest that they must be famous members of the international wisdom community, gathered from various points around the ancient Near East to comfort their distinguished colleague, Job. Who better than they to put forth the basic message of wisdom? Everything axiomatically follows God's great, established plan for this world, so justice must always triumph. As one of them says:

> Can God ever judge men unfairly? Can His sentence be
>   reckoned unjust?
> Your sons must have risen against Him; now they've paid the
>   full price of their sin.
> But you—if in truth you beseech Him, if you plead your own
>   case before God,
> Then surely He will protect you, and pay back your virtue in
>   full.

But after a while, Job is just not buying.

> It's always the same—that's what I say: He kills guilty and
>   guiltless alike.
> If a sudden disaster should strike, He *laughs* at the innocents'
>   downfall.

The earth is surrendered to evil; He blindfolds the eyes of the
    judge.
If He's not the one, then who does it? . . .
                                I'm disgusted with all of
    my life.
Let me give my protest free rein and pour out my bitter
    complaint.
I say to God: Don't convict me until I at least know the charge.
Or are You just pleased with unfairness, oppressing those You
    created, while smiling on champions of wrong? . . .
[And if not,] why *do* You pursue me and decide that I'm guilty of
    sin,
When You know in Your heart that I'm not? But no one can save
    me from You.

Meanwhile, the comforters keep hammering away. Sometimes
their "comfort" takes on a nasty, accusatory tone: Who do you think
you are, Job, to question God's will?

Can you grasp the limits of God, or seize the extent of His being?
You can't reach the summits of heaven or plumb to the depths of
    Sheol,
To measure what's longer than earth, and wider across than the
    sea . . .
But if you direct your mind upward, beseech Him with uplifted
    arms,
If you banish the sins of your past, and give no quarter to evil,
You'll rise again without blemish, being steadied and fearing no
    more,
Forgetting the things that you've suffered. They will pass like a
    swift-flowing stream.

In so saying, the comforters have long-established doctrine on
their side; they repeat philosophical truths that were deemed self-

evident. But Job is really suffering. For him, this debate is not primarily about ideas but about what is happening to him, the ruin of his body day after day:

> But now I'm completely worn out as suffering tightens its grip.
> At nighttime my strength disappears, but my sweats keep on all
>   the same.
> With effort I undo my clothing; my hands try to put on my tunic.
> I've been thrown down to the mud; now I really *am* dust and
>   ashes.
>
> If I bow to You, You don't answer; if I stand, You pay me no
>   mind.
> My torments increase with Your cruelty, pounding at me with
>   full force.
> Then You sweep me up like the wind until my senses desert me.
> I know what awaits me is death. That's where all the living are
>   gathered.
> But must it be gotten with pain? Does one have to suffer to die?
> And *haven't* I wept for that day, poured out my soul for my
>   downfall?
> When I cry, all I get is more suffering, blackness instead of the
>   light.
> Now my insides are never at rest. Misery haunts all my days.

The book of Job goes on for more than forty chapters: the comforters say something, then Job answers them, then they answer back. Frankly, the book could have been twenty or thirty chapters shorter without materially changing the argument: the comforters keep saying the same things, and so does Job. If, nevertheless, the book's author went on and on, he seems to have done so because he himself just couldn't get enough of this tennis match; he loved playing both sides. New examples, new turns of phrases, kept popping into his head: just one more telling metaphor, just one more

145

pithy summary. But finally, the exchanges end when God Himself steps onto the stage. He has the last word in this dispute, in fact, the last five chapters or so. What He says is that no human being, Job included, can begin to fathom Him or the world He created:

> Who is this obscuring the truth with words lacking all under-
> standing?
> Get up on your feet like a man: now *I'll* ask and you give the
> answers.
> Where were you when I made the earth? Did you *see* Me lay its
> foundations?
> Who determined its size—you must know! What measuring
> stick was extended?
> What were its bases sunk into, and who put its cornerstone
> down,
> as the morning stars droned in chorus and the angels of God
> sang their song? . . .
> Have you ever surveyed the whole earth? Tell Me as soon as
> you've seen it.
> What path leads to where the light dwells, and where does the
> darkness reside?
> Can you lead it back to its homeland, return it to where it
> belongs?
> You must know—you were born way back then! You've been
> around for so long . . .

So begins God's lengthy, often sarcastic, response to Job's questioning of His judgment. As noted, this response goes on for several chapters, but its basic message is presented in the opening lines cited above: God created the world and its rules, human beings are Johnny-come-latelies; God knows what humans cannot begin to grasp; God has the power, and humans must accept His decrees. As if to concretize this message (as well as to rectify an injustice), at the very end of the book God restores Job's fortunes and "blessed Job's later years even more than his earlier ones," giving him even greater wealth and a new family of ten children. It seems that neither Job nor his comforters could have had any idea of how things would really turn out.

Despite this happy ending, many modern readers find God's response to Job unsatisfactory, indeed, profoundly unsettling. After all, what kind of an answer is it for Him to pull rank? Couldn't He have actually addressed the question of human suffering, offering some tidbit, some little piece of hope or explanation for generations and generations of sufferers to come? Instead, the answer Job gets is somewhat reminiscent of the catch line of an American radio comedy popular in the 1930s. In it, the comedian Jackie Pearl portrayed a somewhat bombastic baron with a thick German accent.* The show consisted mostly of crude vaudeville one-liners, like:

Straight man: You seem to be effervescent tonight, baron.
Jackie Pearl: Haff you effer seen me ven I effer vasn't?

However, the show's great contribution to American culture (and its relevance to the end of the book of Job) was what the Jackie Pearl character would answer whenever his straight man expressed doubts at one of Jackie's tall tales: "Vas you dere, Charlie?" For several decades, and perhaps even now in some quarters, "Vas you dere, Charlie?" was a quick put-down for any skeptic in any situation. But it is also, in essence, what God tells Job at the end of the book: I created the world and the divine plan that governs it long before you came along. Were you there, Job? Since the answer is no, be quiet!

This answer seems *so* unsatisfactory that some modern biblical scholars refuse to take it seriously. The book of Job must be some sort of enormous parody, they say; God's final answer was meant as a satire. But they are wrong. Like certain other authors of dialogues

---

* He was actually identified as Baron Munchausen (1720–97), who was a famous fibber in real life and later became the archetype of the teller of tall tales.

between two characters, Job's creator wished to have it both ways: he wanted in all sincerity to register Job's complaint, to have his hero ask the sickening question and so uphold its validity. It was, in his view, an altogether justified question. But the answer his book gave to this question was also, in his view, altogether justified; in fact, it seemed to him the only possible answer: what, when you consider the matter, can you really say you *understand* about human existence, about the significance of your own being? "Vas you dere, Charlie?" is really another version of the Iraqi Jew's "God is very big and man is very small." The book of Job only looks like a parody when you inhabit a very different world, one in which man is very big and God is very far away.

Job doesn't say so explicitly, but he appears to be a monotheist—as do his comforters. There is certainly no talk in the book of other heavenly powers capable of countering God's will. But does this book's brand of monotheism offer a satisfactory answer to the sickening question? If you carry monotheism to its logical conclusion, then all the bad things of this world—not only Job's suffering, but the most horrendous things imaginable—must come from God. God is, in the words of the book of Isaiah, "the shaper of light and creator of darkness, the maker of well-being *and creator of evil*" (Isaiah 45:7). When you think about it, there is really nothing theoretically troubling about a Supreme Being who is responsible for both good and bad. In one simple assertion, the "problem of evil" has its answer: all-powerful, inscrutable God creates everything, good and bad, justice and injustice alike. So why not?

Yet it is interesting to note—in keeping with the theme that I have been exploring—how rare such an unflinching attribution of all adversity to God really is, particularly in the Bible. In fact, even the verse from Isaiah just cited contains the hint of another answer to the problem of evil, one that lies in its implied comparison. That is: *just as* God creates both light and darkness, *so too* He also creates both well-being and evil—well-being's opposite. The very juxtaposition of these two assertions seems intended to imply that, just as the first pair is a necessary part of our life on earth, so is the second pair. That is to say, creating only light with no darkness might allow some kind of existence, but certainly nothing resembling what we call life.* Similarly, a world in which there is only unending well-being and no adversity might also be some kind of existence, but it would not be *life,* in which adversity as great as a tsunami or as trivial as a pinprick alternates with everything that is fine and good. In a world in which God brought only good things, what would *not* impugn His goodness? The death of a single human being, or of any creature, indeed, the slightest little illness or fender bender or paper cut would set off a theological cataclysm: how can this world be exclusively controlled by a single deity who does only good? So instead, Isaiah's verse seems to argue, God's goodness is *necessarily* far from absolute: the world has to have at least some adversity in order to be the world. This may be true, and yet, the apologetic character of this assertion is obvious: God does create evil, but it's really for our own good.

Henri Frankfort argued that the rise of Israelite monotheism—which might, theoretically, have left God exclusively responsible for the existence of evil—actually offered a somewhat different explanation for evil's persistence. God tells people what to do, but they don't always obey; when they don't, they are punished, and all manner of bad things happen as a result. In other words, *theomachy* (the conflict of different gods that resulted in our ever-varied human existence) came to be replaced by a new sort of conflict, that of the single, good God's interaction with His disobedient human subjects: evil happens because of what *we* do. And so the Bible says, for example, that the ruins of Sodom and Gomorrah are a potent reminder of the fact that

---

* I don't mean to imply that this comparison was intended to say that all light and no darkness would make human vision impossible—that seems too modern a thought for biblical times. Rather, the idea is that having light all the time would mean that night would never come and human life would become unrecognizable; so too if life consisted of well-being alone.

the inhabitants of that region were "evil and sinners before the LORD" (Genesis 13:13). What exactly occurred in ancient times to turn the site of Sodom into a ruin is not entirely clear, but some geologists have concluded that the area was actually destroyed by an earthquake of significant magnitude (at least 6.8 on the Richter scale). In support of such a hypothesis is Sodom's location, right along the great Syro-African rift, the point at which two tectonic plates (called the Palestinian platelet and the Arabian platelet) are presently, and have been for millennia, sliding past each other in opposite directions. (This may be an apt metaphor for modern Middle Eastern politics, but that's another story.) In short, the destruction of Sodom would no doubt be classified today as some sort of natural catastrophe.

Of course, that is not what the book of Genesis says: the city was destroyed because of the sinfulness of its inhabitants. Interestingly, however, exactly what that sinfulness consisted of is left blank. (Most modern readers associate Sodom's sin with, quite naturally, sodomy, but this is hardly clear from the text itself. In fact, the prophet Ezekiel, who certainly lived closer chronologically to the events at Sodom than we do, said that the inhabitants of Sodom were punished because of their "pride, surfeit of food, and prosperous ease," as a result of which they "did not aid the poor and needy [but] were haughty"—Ezekiel 16:49–50.)[4] But as far as the Genesis narrative was concerned, the precise cause was apparently not that important; all that was important was to attribute Sodom's downfall to "sin" in general. So too for the great flood that struck the earth in the time of Noah:

> The LORD saw how great was man's wickedness on earth, and how every plan devised by his mind was nothing but evil all the time. And the LORD regretted that He had made man on earth, and His heart was saddened. The LORD said, "I will blot out from earth the men whom I created—men together with beasts, creeping things, and birds of the sky, since I regret having made them." But Noah found favor with the LORD. (Genesis 6:5–8)

I like to think of the angel Metatron or some other heavenly copy editor scribbling in the margins of Genesis an editorial query: "Details?" But there are none. People were wicked, the text says, that's all—just like the blanket condemnation of the entire population of Sodom. In the case of the Flood, it is true that the assertion that God "saw how great was man's wickedness on earth" is followed by the specification that people were always making evil plans (even if, apparently, those plans had not yet come to fruition), that is, "every plan devised by [people's] mind[s] was nothing but evil all the time." But does this really explain much more? And how can it be thought to justify the full-scale extinction of "men together with beasts, creeping things, and birds of the sky"? Throughout, there is not one single, specific act or incident that is put forward as the reason for this great flood.[5] Indeed, with both the flood and the destruction of Sodom, there seems to be something rather run-of-the-mill and even unconvincing about the "sinfulness" explanation, the biblical equivalent of "Round up the usual suspects."

In any case, one might well ask if, in the long run, human sinfulness really turns out to be any better an answer to the sickening question, "How can *You* do this?" Wickedness may have caused the great flood and the destruction of Sodom, but how can it explain the death of a newborn baby? Even if that death is somehow deemed to be a punishment of the parents, was not the baby himself or herself an altogether innocent human being? And how far forward can vicarious, or intergenerational, punishment go? The Hebrew Bible itself is somewhat inconsistent on this point, suggesting variously that God can "visit the fathers' sin upon the sons, up to the third and fourth generations of My enemies" (Exodus 20:5, 34:7), whereas elsewhere it says that God will punish the sinner alone, indeed, that penitent sinners will be forgiven (Ezekiel 18:1–9, 21–23; cf. Deuteronomy 24:16).

If the Bible, along with all manner of theologians, both early and late,[6] offered an answer ("human sinfulness") that, on reflection, seems to fail the reality check when it comes to infant deaths and other examples of undeserved suffering, one has to wonder why.

And why, for that matter, those other, well-known explanations? "Those whom He loves God causes to suffer," a rabbinic maxim has it (based on Proverbs 3:12); or suffering in this world is the price of admission to the eternal bliss of the world to come; or suffering in this world is the punishment for sins in a previous life; or suffering that appears unjust only appears so because of human ignorance ("Vas you dere, Charlie?"); and yet others.[7] Why not opt for that most straightforward of answers, the unqualified assertion that evil also comes from God? Monotheism itself would hardly be threatened by such an answer: the fearsome Creator of all is responsible—don't ask why. It is not that such an assertion is entirely absent from the Bible:

> See then that I, I am He; there is no god beside Me.
> I kill and I give life; I wound and I also heal, and no one can
>   escape My power. (Deuteronomy 32:39)

> Come, let us turn to the LORD, for the One who attacks also
>   heals, the One who wounds also bandages. (Hosea 6:1)

But such assertions are rare. Somehow, the Bible usually prefers to ignore the logical consequences of monotheism in favor of the assertion that God is basically good—and then try to reckon with the sickening question in some other way.

How deep religion goes, and how much we ourselves are preprogrammed for it, ultimately touches on the sickening question and how religions respond to it. I have been saying that the perfectly reasonable answer to that question—that evil comes to us directly from God/the gods—is largely rejected by monotheists and polytheists alike, and that this circumstance reflects something basic, perhaps something built into our brains, about right and wrong, just and unjust. Those great heavenly powers cannot be *essentially* wrong or unjust or even indifferent—not because we couldn't stand to think about what would result from such an arrangement (would it be any worse than reality is now?), but because in that stark world of primary colors and yes-or-no, God is neither indifferent nor even sometimes good and sometimes not. That is not the starkness. And in that same world, and by the same token, Little Man cannot be morally indifferent. Notions of what is right and what is wrong, permissible and forbidden, certainly vary from culture to culture across the globe. But no ethnographer has ever found a civilization that does not have such basic distinctions, and this too, it seems to me, is connected to the state of mind which is my subject.

I0

An End to Omens

I am coming to the end of my own personal story, as well as to the end of these thoughts about smallness. I don't suppose anyone has ever chronicled the history of smallness as such, but any such history would probably locate the first, tentative step in the gradual weakening of this state of mind somewhere in humanity's distant past. In fact, as soon as human beings began to gain a greater measure of control over their environment, the old way of conceiving of oneself, and of fitting in to the world, must have already begun to fade. Not all at once, of course, and never completely. (As I wrote in the first chapter, I don't think that there are many people who have *not* experienced a flash of this state of mind at least once or twice.) Still, it is indisputable that nowadays, our sense of smallness is only an occasional flash, something that has otherwise been pushed to the margins of our consciousness. Certainly one important milestone on that path was passed when the great, looming Outside first came to be subdivided into different gods. Now, Little Man was not quite so little; he could at least identify the hidden causes of his own existence and seek to appease them and gain their favor. During this same period, the conditions of human existence were being changed by rapid advances in technology—new tools, new weapons, and eventually agriculture and domesticated animals. These likewise must have had a great deal to do with changing people's outlook on the world and their own

155

sense of self; life simply became less threatening. Much, much later came monotheism. This was a relatively minor matter when compared to the others mentioned (and hardly a universal phenomenon), yet its effect also deserves a place in this history. For monotheists, the world no longer appeared to be in the hands of many divine powers interacting with one another in unpredictable fashion; instead, reality was the product of a single divine will, one that, with effort, could be appealed to and even appeased. What is more, this sole God now no longer entered and left our world, as He did before. Instead, He presided over it in invisible constancy. Human beings still cowered respectfully before the divine, but God's sphere of action now seemed more constrained and foreseeable—less ominous.

Hecataeus of Abdera, a Greek historian who lived at the end of the fourth century BCE, tells an amusing story about a certain march in which he participated during, or just following, Alexander the Great's conquest of the ancient Near East:

> When I was on the march toward the Red Sea, among the escort of Jewish cavalrymen who accompanied us was a certain Mosollamus [Hebrew *Meshullam*], a very intelligent man, robust, and by common consent, the very best of bowmen, whether Greek or barbarian.
>
> This man, noticing that a number of people were now idling on the path and that the whole force was being held up by a seer who was taking the auguries, asked [the seer] why they were stopping. The seer pointed to a certain bird he was observing, and told him that if it stayed in that spot, they would do well to wait around for a while. If it got up and flew forward, then they would be free to proceed; if, however, it flew backward, they were to turn back.
>
> The Jew, without saying a word, drew his bow and shot, hitting the bird and killing it. The seer and some of the others became

indignant and began heaping curses on him. "What are you poor people getting so upset about?" he asked. Then, picking up the bird in his hands, he said: "How could any sound information about our journey have been provided by this poor creature, who was unable to make provision for his own safety? For if he had any gift for divination, he never would have come to this place, for fear of being killed by an arrow from Mosollamus the Jew."

Mosollamus, clearly, was someone who had been cured of the fear of omens, and if his being a Jew had anything to do with it (as Hecataeus may be implying), one might chalk this up to the interesting turn that Judaism had taken by his time.

Biblical scholars are far from certain when monotheism—the belief that there is only one God in the world, and that, therefore, there is only one divine will that determines all of reality—began to be accepted. Careful scrutiny of the Bible itself, as well as of the writings of ancient Israel's neighboring civilizations, has made it clear that this belief (or realization) came into existence only after a while. Thus, despite a later tradition hallowed by Jews, Christians, and Muslims alike, there is really no indication in the Bible that Abraham (or, for that matter, Isaac or Jacob) maintained that there is only one God; He is certainly said to have been *their* God, but that implies nothing about monotheism. Likewise, the Ten Commandments delivered by Moses at Mount Sinai included one provision that stated, "You shall have no other gods *before Me* . . ." This phrase is somewhat ambiguous: it could mean "in My presence," or it might even mean "taking precedence over Me." But it certainly doesn't mean, "Worshiping any other god is nonsense, since I am the only one."

But Israel did, eventually, become monotheistic. This didn't happen all at once, and even after monotheism had apparently been adopted as doctrine in some circles, Israel's prophets still found it necessary for some centuries to rebuke the people for backsliding into the worship of Baal or Ashtoret. In the end, however, the backsliding just stopped. The author of the (apocryphal) book of Judith, writing in the third or second century BCE, had its heroine assert: "For never in our generation nor in these present days has there been any tribe or family of people or city of ours which worshiped gods made by [human] hands . . . We know no other God but Him" (Judith 8:18, 20). This is probably (though not certainly) an accurate reflection of the author's own world.

Monotheism (Jewish, Christian, and Muslim) soon spread over much of the rest of the globe—true, sometimes at sword point, but often not. When confronted with monotheism for the first time, polytheists and animists all over the world frequently reacted (if their own accounts are to be believed) with: "Sure! Why didn't I think of that?" But what *was* the appeal of believing in only one God? On reflection, it seems counterintuitive. After all, the world itself is composed of so many different things. The sun moves through the sky, then the moon shows up; the seasons change, with spring supplanting winter; there is ample rain sometimes, but at other times drought; war brings victory or defeat. As was seen in the previous chapter, people had always fixed on the variegated nature of human life to suggest that there are competing forces in heaven, different gods fighting it out up there—with us humans reaping the fruits or suffering the consequences. What was the appeal of an ideology that claimed that such opposites came from a single divine source?

Part of the answer seems to lie in the change that monotheism suggested to potential converts about the very nature of divinity. A single God who was responsible for everything was indeed a great God, greater than any previously imagined: He ruled simultaneously over land and sea, heaven and earth; He cared for the fate not of thousands, but of millions. (An ongoing, thorny problem was: how could such a universal deity also be the God of, specifically, one people, and a pretty small one at that? But that is not our concern here.) Next to Him, rain gods, war gods, harvest gods, and so forth seemed like little godlings. Worshiping them when such a great God existed seemed utterly foolish. When his shipmates ask Jonah who he is, " 'I am a Hebrew,' he replied, 'I worship the LORD, the God of Heaven, who made both sea and land,' and the men were greatly terrified."

This is certainly not the whole story, but in any case, this sole God's greatness was at first expressed in His size: the human-sized, optical-illusion God who stood just behind the curtain of the ordinary came to be conceived of as considerably more than human-sized. In the book of Isaiah, God asks rhetorically: "The heavens are My throne, and the earth a little stool for My feet; where then is the house/temple that you would build for Me—where is My dwelling place?" Too big to be contained means very big indeed. But soon, this bigness turned out to really be omnipresence: now it was clear that God was simply everywhere all at once. And omnipresence also meant omniscience: since God was everywhere, there could be nothing in the world, nothing that humans did or even thought, that He did not know.

These things are never said outright in the Hebrew Bible, but they soon became common knowledge, and one of their consequences was to make the earth a far less ominous place. Once it was understood that God was everywhere all at once, He could no longer cross the curtain into our world; He was there already, everywhere. This made life in His presence entirely different from the earlier moments of visitation: His being everywhere seemed to mean that He was never somewhere in particular. Thus, omnipresence (though this may sound paradoxical) kept God at arm's length, kept the starkness at arm's length. Since He would no longer show up at your tent in the guise of three men, you never risked actually being physically *confronted;* instead, He would cause things to happen from a distance, without any physical intervention on His part. In this sense, God would henceforth be remote; that is why it is only after this change that people are said to be "in search of God."

As I have already suggested, this great shift did not happen overnight, nor was it ever as complete as I am making out. I used to think that it was only Christianity that had, in a sense, actually combined the old, human-sized deity of those early biblical texts with the omnipresent, omniscient deity of later Judaism; wasn't this implicit in the Nicene doctrine of the Trinity? But Judaism, too, was reluctant to give up the God of old, who is frequently compared in rabbinic writings to a human king and regularly depicted in prayer and song as seated on a heavenly throne surrounded by His angel attendants. Indeed, the utterly transcendent deity was stoutly resisted, especially by Jewish and Christian mystics, long into the Middle Ages and beyond. But slowly, the way ordinary people thought about God became very different from what it had been, and this more distant Deity brought with Him a lower level of anxiety. The other, "stark," visionary way of seeing began to recede.[1]

This gradual change is reflected as well in the way people thought about signs and omens. Since this single, all-powerful Deity was now the final arbiter in all things, what was the point of scrutinizing the usual clues about the future? In the end, He would decide; so pray to Him, find favor with Him, and everything will turn out well. The author of the nonbiblical *Book of Jubilees,* a Jew who wrote around the year 200 BCE, retold much of the book of Genesis in his own words, with more than a few of his own additions. Here is his version of what Abraham came to think about omens:

Abra[ha]m sat at night—at the beginning of the seventh month—to observe the stars from evening to dawn in order to see what would be the character of the year with respect to the rains. He was sitting and observing by himself when a voice came to his mind and he said: "All the signs of the stars and the signs of the moon and the sun—all are under the Lord's control. Why should I be investigating [them]? If He wishes He will make it rain in the morning and evening: and if He wishes, He will not make it fall. Everything is under his control." That night he prayed and said: "My God, my God, God most High, You alone are my God. You have created everything: everything that was and has been is the product of your hands. You and your lordship I have chosen. Save me from the power of the evil spirits who rule the thoughts of people's minds. May they not mislead me from following you, my God. Do establish me and my posterity forever. May we not go astray from now until eternity."

But old ways die slowly. Even Abraham, in this passage, asks for protection against the "evil spirits." God may be the Supreme Being, but there are lesser forces from "the other side" who can still make life miserable; like bacteria, the evil spirits were everywhere in the second century, and they could infiltrate a person's brain and "rule the thoughts of people's minds." Witchcraft, magic, and occult forces were still definitely part of the world. One way to oppose them was to enlist occult forces on your own.

The Pentateuch had officially banned magicians, wizards, mediums, and the like (Exodus 22:17, Leviticus 19:26, Deuteronomy 18:10–14, etc.), but that is probably only a good indication that such figures were indeed welcomed in some quarters. The book of 1 Samuel recounts, for example, how King Saul, desperate for an oracle about a coming battle, goes to a medium in order to summon the prophet Samuel from the dead; though unhappy with being roused, Samuel does indeed provide the requested oracle. A law in Leviticus 19:14 says, "You shall not curse the deaf or place a stumbling block before the blind." Cursing in biblical times meant not simply venting your anger on someone, but seeking to hurt him with the occult power of your words. (If cursing is thus bad, one might ask, why not forbid it altogether? Apparently such a global prohibition was simply unreasonable; cursing was just part of life.) As for not cursing the deaf, however, the reason is plain. Being deaf, the victim has no way to defend himself against your curse or even to know about it; thus, by cursing him you are taking unfair advantage, just as you would be taking unfair advantage of the blind person if you put a physical stumbling block in front of him.

What specific measures could be used to ward off curses, evil spirits, and other unseen enemies? One centuries-old means was to inscribe a counteracting phrase or passage on an amulet, which could then be kept in the house or carried about on one's person for protection. Here, for example, is a sixth- or seventh-century BCE inscription in Aramaic from Arslan Tash, in northern Syria:

> An incantation against flying demonesses, the curse of Sasm son
> of Padrish.
> Call out these things and say to the she-stranglers:
> Any house that I enter, you are not to enter,
> and in any courtyard that I walk, you are not to walk.
> An eternal agreement has been established for us.
> [The god] Ashur has established it for us, along with all the gods
> and the head[s] of the assembly of all the holy ones.
> Through the agreement of [i.e., witnessed by] heaven and earth,
> Through the bond of [the god] Horon's wife, who always speaks
> the truth,
> and *her* seven co-wives and the eight wives of Baʿal . . . [2]

In late biblical times, long after the rise of monotheism, people still recited special prayers and incantations to ward off evil spirits and the like; the practice is well attested in the Dead Sea Scrolls. Indeed, at least one of our canonical psalms was used for such "apotropaic purposes," that is, to counteract evil. The potential victim had simply to recite these words:

> One who dwells in the Eternal's protection, who remains in the
> Almighty's keeping,
> will say of the LORD, "He is my refuge and fortress, the God in
> whom I put my trust."
> For He will save you from the hunter's snare, [that is,] from a
> word that brings destruction.
> He will cover you with His pinions, and under His wings you
> will shelter; His faithfulness is a shield and buckler.

So you need not cringe in nighttime terror—not from an arrow
      that flies during the day,
nor from a word that slips about through the darkness, nor from
      an evil spirit that hunts in broad daylight. (Psalm 91: 1–6)

Such means were not used only for defensive purposes. You could also go on the offensive by inscribing a curse on a statuette of someone you wished to harm, or on an "execration bowl"; either would then be ritually smashed, thereby releasing the power of your curse and, in effect, letting it loose.[3] A similar, ancient form of cursing (called in Greek "making a *katadesmos*" or, in Latin, a *defixio*) has been widely evidenced in excavations all over the Greco-Roman world. A curse would be inscribed on a small sheet of lead, then folded up, pierced with a nail made out of bronze or iron, and finally placed at some strategically significant locale, such as in a tomb, or dropped into a vital body of water, like a well, a bath, or a fountain. The inscriptions said things like:

> Just as you, Theonnastos [the dead person with whom the inscription was buried] are powerless in the movement of your hands, your feet, your body . . . so too may Zoilos be powerless to come to Antheira, and in the same way Antheira [to] Zoilos.

or

> Just as this lead is buried . . . so too may you [the corpse] utterly bury the works, the household, the affections, and everything else of Zoilos.

(Poor Zoilos!)

Sometimes such *defixiones* were not used for cursing, but in order to get the love of your life to take an interest in you:

> Don't ignore these names, *nekudaimon* [spirit of the dead], but arouse yourself and go to every place where Matrona is, whom

Tagene bore. You have her *ousia* [essence, identity]. Go to her and seize her sleep, her drink, her food, and do not allow Matrona (whom Tagene bore, whose *ousia* you have) to have love or intercourse with any other man, except Theodoros, whom Techosis bore. Drag Matrona by her hair, by her guts, by her soul, by her heart until she comes to Theodoros and make her inseparable from me until death, night and day, for every hour of time. Immediately, immediately; quickly, quickly; now, now.[4]

Such resorts to the occult were not uncommon in far later times, but long before they began to disappear, people were already thinking of them as belonging to a special realm, the world of the supernatural. This in itself bespeaks a measure of human control, since it implies that *that* world is separate and somewhat unusual: most of the time things do not belong to the occult realm, which is to say, most of the time things are normal. Of course, the actual categories of *natural* versus *supernatural* come still later (in Europe, only in the late Middle Ages). Evans-Pritchard describes a somewhat foggier reckoning with this distinction among the Azande:

It is often asked whether primitive people distinguish between the natural and the supernatural, and the query may here be answered in a preliminary manner . . .

The question as it stands may mean: do primitive peoples distinguish between the natural and the supernatural in the abstract? We have a notion of an ordered world conforming to what we call natural laws, but some people in our society [also] believe that mysterious things can happen which cannot be accounted for by reference to natural laws and which therefore are held to transcend them, and we call these happenings supernatural. To us, supernatural means very much the same as abnormal or extraordinary.

Azande certainly have no such notions of reality. They have no conceptions of the "natural" as we understand it, and therefore neither of the "supernatural" as we understand it. But . . .

Azande undoubtedly perceive a difference between what we consider the workings of nature on the one hand and the workings of magic and ghosts and witchcraft on the other hand, though in the absence of a formulated doctrine of natural law they do not, and cannot, express the difference as we express it.[5]

This was true in ancient Israel as well: there was no formulated theory of the supernatural, but even its potentially positive side, God's crossing over into the human realm, carried with it a definite anxiety; there was nothing comfortable about the eerie proximity. People nowadays generally do not notice that biblical figures back then are almost never said to be "in search of God." Quite the contrary! Unless desperately ill or otherwise in need of urgent help, they preferred not to encounter God at all, and even then, they wished only to be helped long enough to overcome their difficulty and then slip back into their former anonymity; an ongoing "relationship" with God (to use the term often employed by today's clergypeople) was no one's goal in biblical times. At Mount Sinai, when God came down to make his eternal covenant with Israel, designating them as his "special treasure," the people "fell back and stood at a distance. 'You be the one to speak to us,' they said to Moses, 'and we will obey—but don't let God speak to us, lest we die.'" Before this, even Israel's great spiritual leaders, Abraham and Sarah, Jacob, and Moses himself all react with fear when first confronted by God or an angel. It would have been better for all concerned, they seem to feel, if He had stayed on the other side of the curtain.

The omens continued to exist long after Europe was Christianized; indeed, Christianity was often the omens' close friend, a frequent feature in tales of the saints. But then, slowly at first, their sphere of influence began to shrink. The whole realm of the supernatural underwent a marked contraction in Western Europe—not, as one might suppose, with the scientific revolution, but well before it, during the period of, roughly, 1000 to 1500 of the common era.⁶ The supernatural of course continued to exist, but, as I mentioned, the very act of distinguishing the natural from the supernatural was a distinction that bespoke mankind's growing power over occult forces.

One indication of this change is the phenomenon of "trial by ordeal." In many societies, supernatural means were used to determine a person's guilt or innocence, or the appropriateness or inappropriateness of a given course of action: lots were cast, entrails were scrutinized, arrows were shot, and so forth, and the results determined what was to be done. This was not, it should be stressed, like our flipping a coin nowadays, where the utterly random nature of the outcome is generally recognized by the participants. Instead, the results here were taken to be an expression of the divine will. In the trial by ordeal, the person on trial was subjected to some dangerous or painful procedure—walking over hot coals or the like—and was deemed to be guilty or innocent depending on the results. A mild form of this sort of thing is found even in biblical law: A woman suspected by her husband of adultery (without, however, his being able to prove the charge in court) was brought to the temple, where the priest would mix some of the earth that was on the sanctuary floor with water in an earthenware vessel. He would then recite:

> "If no [other] man has slept with you and if you have not gone astray in defilement while married to your husband, may you be safe from harm from this water of bitterness . . . But if you *have* gone astray . . . may the LORD make you a curse and an imprecation among your people, with the LORD causing your thigh to sag and your belly to be distended." (Numbers 5:19–21)

To this the woman would answer, "Amen, amen," and then drink the water. If she was guilty, she would indeed suffer the physical effects mentioned, but if she was innocent, she would be unharmed, in fact (it was specified), she would be able to conceive children. There is no indication that this trial by ordeal was ever a common practice, and it was in any case officially abolished in Judaism in the first century CE (Mishnah *Sotah* 9:9). Before that time, one rabbinic account (perhaps apocryphal) reports an unfortunate case involving twin sisters. The innocent one dressed up in the other sister's clothes, went to the temple, and drank the brew; she walked away unharmed. However, justice was not foiled! When the guilty sister went to kiss her helpful sibling in thanks, she inadvertently inhaled some of the vapors still emitting from her sister's mouth and died on the spot.[7]

Christian trials by ordeal continued long after this time, in fact, well into the Middle Ages. And they were no joke: indeed, they were known by the somewhat more ominous name of "the Judgment of God" (*iudicium Dei*). The accused, or one of the parties in a civil suit, would have to carry a red-hot iron a certain distance, or else pick up a pebble from out of a boiling cauldron, or be thrown into a pool of cold water or a rushing stream. If, in the case of the red-hot iron or the boiling water, the person's hand healed within a prescribed time period (usually three days), he or she was determined to have passed the test. Oddly enough, being thrown into the cold water worked in what might seem the opposite way. If the person floated, this was a sure sign of guilt; only by sinking was the test passed! (What good did it do to pass under such circumstances? Usually, the person undergoing the test had a rope attached to his or her body and was thus rescued before actually drowning.)

The interesting thing is that such trials virtually disappeared from Western Europe by the year 1300, and it seems that this was part of a wider trend that limited (but certainly did not eliminate entirely) the role of the supernatural in human affairs. It may not be a coincidence that this was also the time when the writings of Plato and Aristotle, as well as other Greek scientific and mathematical treatises, were making their way into Latin, often via earlier translations into Arabic. (Greek had been largely unknown in Western Europe.) A whole new attitude to the formerly supernatural world was emerging, what the sociologist Max Weber called "breaking the magic spell" of the world.[8] The uncanny was receding.

✦ ✦ ✦

The disappearance of miraculous happenings is another symptom of this same change in mentality. There are lots of miracles in the Bible, and biblical Hebrew uses different words to describe them; frequently they are called "signs" (*'otot* or, in later Hebrew, *nissim*) and "wonders" (*mofetim, nifla'ot*). These and other terms seem to be used more or less interchangeably, and all sorts of instances of the miraculous were, apparently, accepted unquestioningly: as a tenth-century BCE bumper sticker might have put it, "Miracles happen." Nowadays, of course, readers of the Bible are often troubled by such narratives as that of the Ten Plagues that struck the Egyptians in the book of Exodus, or the New Testament account of the raising of Lazarus from the dead—surely there must be some rational, scientific explanation for what really happened! And indeed, such explanations are put forward in abundance. Thus, the Ten Plagues really began, some modern interpreters suggest, with an infestation of red algae in the Nile, which caused the river to have a dark red appearance and so "turn to blood." Soon, these undrinkable waters forced the Nile frogs to leave their river habitat and seek refuge in people's houses, where they died (the second plague). In time, swarms of insects (the fourth plague) were attracted by the frog corpses; and so on. As for Lazarus, he wasn't really dead; modern heart massage or mouth-to-mouth respiration similarly returns apparently lifeless corpses to normal functioning, and that must have been the case with him as well.

The rationalizing of the formerly miraculous has a long history, but scholars have noted one milestone along this path in the medieval attempt to distinguish the "truly miraculous" from things that merely appear so because they are not fully understood. This distinction was gaining currency precisely at the time when people's guilt or innocence stopped being tested with red-hot irons or a dip in a fast-running stream. As one scholar has noted, "By the thirteenth century, theologians and natural philosophers agreed that *mirabilia* ["wonders," corresponding to the Hebrew terms *mofetim* and *nifla'ot* mentioned earlier] included all things at which we might feel wonder because we did not understand, but that *miracula* [miracles] included only those things which were beyond nature and hence performed only by God."[9]

Another indication of this gradual shift in outlook brings us a little closer to the realm of modern science. What causes an eclipse of the sun or the moon? This is an interesting case of the supernatural, because actually, people had known since ancient times that eclipses all had to do with the alignment of the sun, the moon, and the earth.[10] Indeed, ancient Babylonians and Greeks had worked out the basic cycle of years governing their occurrence. Isidore of Seville (c. 560– 636), whose *Etymologies* served as a learned encyclopedia from his time well into the succeeding centuries, summed up the matter in a few words: "The moon suffers an eclipse if the shadow of the earth comes between it and the sun," while the sun is eclipsed "when the new moon is in line with the sun and obstructs and obscures it" (*Etymologies* 3:53–58).

But causality is a tricky concept. The Azande and the Nuer (both studied by Evans-Pritchard) may not be expert in eclipses, but they understand perfectly well the concatenation of meteorological events that brings about a failed harvest, for example. For them, however, mentioning a drought or excessive rainfall is simply a further description of what happened; it still does not tell you *why* it happened. The same way of looking at things surrounded people's attitudes toward eclipses in the Middle Ages. Despite what Isidore of Seville had said and what, presumably, filtered down to the common folk, people regularly used to yell at the moon in order to assist her in her travail during an eclipse.

Yelling at the moon is attested in numerous medieval sources. *Vince luna* ("Conquer, moon!") was one thing people shouted. Many of the common folk believed that the ultimate (rather than immediate) cause of the eclipse was witchcraft or sorcery: the shouting, therefore, was aimed at undoing the magicians' evil rather than addressed to the moon itself. The Church was naturally opposed to this practice. What was, in its view, part of God's well-ordered universe required no help from humans down below. "When the moon is darkened," warned Eligius, bishop of Noyon in the seventh century, "no one should dare to utter shouts, because it becomes dark at specific times at God's command." But the shouting continued. Hrabanus Maurus, the great encyclopedist of the ninth century, mentions one night of an eclipse, when "such a great shouting arose among the people that its irreligious sound penetrated to the heavens." Inquiring the next day, he found eyewitnesses, one of whom reported having heard the bellowing of warlike horns during the eclipse, another the grunting of pigs; a third said he had seen people shooting spears and arrows at the moon—apparently in an attempt to defend it against its attackers. Referring to the solar eclipse of 990 CE, Thietmar of Merseburg, a German bishop and chronicler, wrote: "I urge all Christians that they should truly believe that this does not happen on account of some incantations by wicked women, nor by eating, and it cannot be helped by any action in this world." Even acceptance of the mechanical understanding of what causes eclipses did not prevent people from continuing to regard their occurrence as a "sign"— in fact, *signum* was a regular term used to refer to an eclipse. In other words, some people simultaneously maintained that eclipses "were signs *as well as* regular physical phenomena—predictive as well as predictable."[11]

So the great march of progress, and in particular the change in mentality that ultimately affected the very way that we conceive of ourselves, seems to have been a thing of fits and starts. Mosollamus the Jew may not have been afraid of omens, and the author of *Jubilees* may have had Abraham put his faith in the one true God and shrugged off astrological signs as bunk. But other people continued to yell at the moon during a lunar eclipse long after its physical causes had been properly explained. Their actions, as well as the persistence of signs and wonders in other domains, indicate that it was not scientific information that made the crucial difference between a world full of miracles and a clockwork universe. Rather, it seems to have been a matter of orientation, a whole turn of mind, that changed very unevenly, and over a very long period of time. In seventeenth-century England, Shakespeare had one of his characters observe, not without a tinge of regret:

> They say miracles are past; and we have our philosophical persons [that is, scientists], to make modern and familiar, things supernatural and causeless. Hence is it that we make trifles of terrors, ensconcing ourselves into seeming knowledge, when we should submit ourselves to an unknown fear. (*All's Well That Ends Well,* 2.3)

But long after Shakespeare's time, people were still submitting themselves "to an unknown fear"; indeed, omens and occult signs have always demonstrated a surprising staying power.

The modern French folklorist Anatole Le Braz knew well the anxiety that omens bring; he described some of them in a memoir of his childhood in southern Brittany, *The Legend of Death Among the Armorican Bretons* (1902).

> Certain people have, more than others, *the gift of sight.* When I was young, people still used to point with their finger—with a kind of stifled dread—at those who were endowed with this mysterious power. *"Hennes hen eus ar pouar,"* they would say ("That one has the power!") . . .
>
> Hearing something fall and then break—a bowl, a plate, or a glass—was a sign of the death of some relative, or of a friend who was traveling. The carpenters who make coffins know in advance if someone in the area is going to die that day or that night: the wooden planks tell them by banging noisily against each other in the loft.

In the region of Paimpol, sailors' wives who haven't had word of their husbands for some time will make a pilgrimage to Saint-Loup-le-Petit (*Sa-Loup-ar-Bihan*). [There] they light the candle that they have brought specially at the feet of the saint. If the husband is all right, the candle burns lustily. But if the husband is dead, the candle flickers listlessly, off and on, and then suddenly goes out.

Often, the sick person himself—or rather, as people say, his *Expérience* (his double)—is the one who announces his imminent death. In such a case he will be wearing the strangest disguise or get-up, showing himself in the form of a black or white animal, depending on whether he is to be saved or lost in the other world.

A woman about to die was spotted in her nightshirt sitting on the branch of an apple tree not far from her home precisely at the moment when she herself was inside, starting her last death-throes.

When someone suddenly shudders for no apparent reason, people generally say that it is because the Ankou (Death) has just passed by. When someone calls out all of a sudden, or if you touch something unexpectedly, do you instinctively jump? That is because death, which had just been about to fall on you, has left you in order to take hold of someone else. If one feels one's eyes unexpectedly well up with tears, that is a sure sign that people soon will be mourning someone from one's own family.[12]

But this anxiety, though it still persists here and there, has become indisputably rarer in our world than it was even a century ago. Some people may still take the astrology column in their daily newspaper seriously, and many businessmen still have a lucky suit or a lucky tie; but the world is generally far less ominous than it used to be, and I think that we humans are correspondingly *bigger* as a result. There are few signs or omens anymore that send us into a state of nervous

An End to Omens

apprehension. In fact, almost the sole remnant of that very ancient mentality in the world of most of us today is the way we feel about cancer: it is still potent magic. In many languages, although the word *cancer* is well known, people avoid using it in ordinary speech. "He's very, very tired," they say in my in-laws' part of France, while "he has the sickness" is common in Israel, and no doubt elsewhere. (The reason is simple. Saying the actual word might cause it to come into existence—in you or in the person you're talking to—or, at the very least, it may hasten the end of the person you're discussing.) Until recently the *New York Times* obituaries used to say, ". . . after a long illness." Doctors themselves try to let patients down easy by avoiding the c-word, or even "tumor": instead, what is discovered is a "slight growth," an "unusual polyp," "a lesion," an "irregularity that should be checked." Despite all clinical evidence to the contrary, many people avoid shaking a cancer sufferer's hand or even being under the same roof with him or her for any extended period. Meanwhile we scrutinize our own bodies for cancer's faint signature. True, this is not like looking for magical omens: real lumps or a slight, tingling pain over the last few weeks can indeed indicate trouble ahead. But this is precisely the same sort of anxiety that people used to feel about all kinds of things in the world. There were warnings everywhere, and woe to him who did not heed them.

The anthropologist Clifford Geertz reported on what happened in Java when "a peculiarly shaped, rather large toadstool" grew up in someone's house in the space of a few days ("or, some said, a few hours"). People came from miles around to see it.

Toadstools play about the same role in Javanese life as they do in ours, and in the ordinary course of things Javanese have about as much interest in them as we do. It was just that this one was "odd," "strange," "uncanny"—*aneh*. And the odd, strange, and uncanny must be accounted for—or again, the conviction it *could be accounted for* sustained. One does not shrug off a toadstool which grows five times as fast as a toadstool has a right to grow.[13]

Reading this, I wondered what it would take in most Western countries to attract people from miles around to view a toadstool (or, to use the more common term today, a mushroom). I doubt that Americans would go to see one just because it had grown up quickly. It might get written up in the local newspaper (though probably not), and even then, "That's a matter for biologists, plant physiologists," we would say. "No doubt it has something to do with a growth gene gone haywire, or with the soil, or something." Which is to say, I think, that we are no longer on the lookout for messages in most of what makes up our daily lives. True, a mushroom that grew up in the likeness of the Virgin Mary, or appeared to have a representation of the crucifixion naturally inscribed on its skin—this might indeed bring the people out, if not in the somewhat blasé U.S., then at least in some of the more traditionally religious populations south of the border. But this too is, I think, just another way of saying that our sense of the ominous has shrunk down to a very few domains. For some (but rather few), a "religious" omen like an inscribed mushroom might require explanation and/or hold out the promise of a revelation or mystical cure if visited in person. But for many others, even such a freak of nature has little draw. For them, the ominous is really down to avoiding words like "cancer."

When I was a little boy, my German-speaking grandmother would mutter something whenever she picked up my baby sister or told my mother what a handsome son she had. For a long time I thought that what she was muttering was in Hebrew, until I knew enough German to recognize the word *unberufen,* which literally means "not summoned up." It was a shorthand way of saying, "Even though I am praising this child, let the Evil Eye not take an interest in him as a result, having been summoned up by my words." She was not, as best I know, a superstitious woman, and if asked she probably would have professed no belief whatsoever in the Evil Eye. I wonder if she would still be saying *unberufen* if she were alive today. I doubt it. It may have lasted a long time, but this manifestation of the ominous, like most others, is today definitely in retreat.

One aspect of the overall evolution in the way that people conceive of the self has been traced by the French cultural historian Philippe Ariès, who focused his study on the history of how people think about death (in general, as well as about their own death in particular)—starting from late antiquity and ending up in present-day America.[14] Centuries ago, he argued, death was a "domesticated" and tame affair. People knew they were going to die, and that was that. In fact, ancient texts often represented the dying person as actively involved in his own passing. It started with his foreseeing that he was about to die—often thanks to an omen or some other supernatural means. Death was now approaching, and so the person had to take the proper preparatory steps.

This is evidenced in numerous ancient texts, including several famous passages in the Hebrew Bible. In one, for example, Jacob tells his son Joseph, "I myself am soon to die, but God will be with you and bring you again to the land of your ancestors." Whereupon he assembles his children and grandchildren in order to reveal the future to them, since the dying have a unique view of things to come: "Gather around that I may tell you what will happen to you in days to come." Having finished his predictions, "Jacob ended his charge to his sons [and] drew up his feet into the bed, breathed his last, and was gathered to his fathers" (Genesis 48:21, 49:1, 33). Such was an orderly death in the olden days. An early, postbiblical book, *The Testaments of the Twelve Patriarchs,* reproduces the same pattern: each of Jacob's twelve sons foresees his death and summons his descendents for a final moral lesson before dying. Sometimes there is no outward sign that death is near—as in the case of Naphtali:

When his sons met together in the seventh month, on the first day of the month, when he was in good health, he made a feast for them. After he woke up the next morning, he said to them, "I am about to die." But they did not believe him . . .

Nevertheless, the dying man himself always knows his end is near, and this is just the first indication of his controlling role.

As for *how* people died, it was, according to these same texts, altogether straightforward and unsentimental. Here, for example, is the same Naphtali's passing:

> And having commanded them many such things as these, he [Naphtali] summoned them [his sons] to take up his bones to Hebron and bury him with his fathers. And after eating and drinking with them in good humor, he covered his face and died. And his sons did according to all that their father Naphtali had commanded them.

Aaron, Moses' brother, is said to have enjoyed a similarly tame death:

> Moses said to him: "Enter this cave," and he entered. "Stretch out your arms," and he did so. "Stretch out your legs," and he did so. "Close your mouth," and he did so. "Close your eyes," and he did so. At that point Moses said to himself, "Happy the one who dies such a death." (*Sifrei* Deuteronomy 339)

In Christian Europe during the early Middle Ages, the pattern was much the same. When the end at last arrived, there were certain steps to be followed. The dying person lay down, head facing Jerusalem, and spread out his arms in the form of a cross. He first lamented his own dying, then he officially pardoned his friends, many of whom were surrounding his deathbed. The next step was to pray to God, admitting his guilt for sins he had committed in his life. This was followed by the *commendatio animae,* whereby the dying person presented his soul to God, asking Him to save it from all peril. Here is the simple text of an early Christian *commendatio:*

Deliver, O Lord, the soul of thy servant, as you delivered Enoch and Elijah from the common death,* as you delivered Noah from the flood, as you delivered Abraham by leading him out of Ur of the Chaldeans, as you delivered Job from his afflictions, Isaac from the hands of his father Abraham, Lot from the flames of Sodom, Moses from the hand of Pharaoh, king of Egypt, Daniel from the lions' den, the three young Hebrews from the fiery furnace, Susanna from a false accusation, David from the hands of Saul and Goliath, Saint Peter and Saint Paul from their prison, and the blessed virgin Saint Thecla from three horrible torments.[15]

After the *commendatio* came absolution, delivered by the priest; the priest then read psalms, burned incense, and sprinkled the dying man's body with holy water. All this was an altogether public event, with relatives and friends, including women and small children, surrounding the deathbed. People "took death calmly," Ariès stresses: "they were as familiar with the actual dead as they were familiarized with the idea of their own death." Every living person was "acutely aware that he had merely been given a stay of execution, that this period would be a brief one, and that death was always present within him, shattering his ambitions and poisoning his pleasures."[16] This frank realism was simply part of the human condition. Along the same lines, the Venerable Bede, an early medieval English theologian and historian, mentions a metaphor for human existence apparently common in his time: A sparrow flies into a banquet hall through an opening under the roof. For a few minutes he is out of the cold and darkness outside, and he flaps about merrily above the revelers. But then he flies out again on the other side, back into the cold.[17]

As time went on, however, things began to change. The first change Ariès noticed was that, at a certain point in the Middle

---

* Ancient tradition, based on the biblical text, held that both Enoch and Elijah had ascended bodily into heaven and had thus escaped death entirely, continuing to live "up there" to eternity. None of the others in this catalogue enjoyed a similar fate, but all were saved ("delivered") by God in one incident or another during their lifetimes.

Ages, death ceased to be tame. Paintings and sculpted representations of the Last Judgment (sometimes called "dooms") had always been around, but now they began to take on a more fearsome aspect. The day of a person's death was conflated with the judgment of his soul—it was thus an all-or-nothing occasion, full of terrors. Eventually, learned writers even began to compose manuals entitled "The Art of Dying" or "The Art of Dying Well," which instructed their readers on the procedures to be followed in order to ensure the best outcome of their last, fateful day. At the same time, representations of death became more graphic. The metaphorical figure of Death came to be depicted in paintings as a half-decomposed corpse. This is also the time of the *danse macabre:*

> The dead lead the dance: indeed, they are the only ones dancing. Each couple consists of a naked mummy, rotting, sexless, and highly animated, and a man or a woman, dressed according to his or her social condition and paralyzed by surprise. Death holds out its hand to the living person whom it will draw along with it, but who has not yet obeyed the summons. The art lies in the contrast between the rhythm of the dead and the rigidity of the living. The moral purpose was to remind the viewer both of the uncertainty of the hour of death and of the equality of all people in the face of death.[18]

There are a few representations of the *danse macabre* in Judaism, but medieval Hebrew poems sometimes similarly stress the fearsome side of the day of death.[19] Some of these poems are still recited in synagogues today. Here, for example, is Judah b. Samuel ibn Balam's eleventh-century vision of a person's last hours:

> What can one say? How can one plead? With what words put
>   forth one's case?
> A creature of dust to dust will return; the dirt will be piled on his
>   face—

Then what can he offer his Maker, and how can the thing be
> arranged?
All his words and his deeds are recorded in a book that can never
> be changed.
"Let us fall into the hand of the Lord, for great are his mercies."

A similar note was struck by his rough contemporary, the philosopher and poet Solomon ibn Gabirol. I have not written his exact dates because they are not certain: he seems to have been born around 1020 and to have died in the late 1050s. If so, he had a surprisingly short life, dying, according to most accounts, sometime between the ages of 35 and 38. During much of his life he was plagued by illness; did his description of a man's last days (written in the "rhyming prose" style of medieval Hebrew and Arabic) reflect his own physical suffering?

As his pain increases, respect for him ceases, until even children
> scorn him aloud; little boys order him about.
He becomes a burden to his own; to his former friends he's now
> unknown,
and when his time comes and he leaves his home, it is for a far
> smaller one, dug into loam;
he trades purple robes and fine brocade for a living, creeping
> cloak that's made
of maggots and worms. There he will stay, melting back into dirt
> with each passing day.

On the same theme, the greatest medieval Hebrew poet, Yehudah ha-Levi (ca. 1075–1141), presented his own, almost ghoulish picture of death:

How can a man   whose sins demand   sure punishment
> ask for surcease?
A man who's stained   with crimes unnamed,   uncounted
> wrongs, hope for release?

179

No one is saved   from a filthy grave   with maggots and
    worms all around;
Yet still he's proud   and boasts aloud   of things that soon
    will not be found;
He chases fame,   the world's acclaim,   but can't remember
    why or what,
forgets the day   when none can say   "Let's put it off; I'd
    rather not."
The day when account books are open,   and forgotten things
    at last come home:
"Mercy and forgiveness are the Lord's alone."

He finds relief   from future grief   in what he owns and
    all he's bought,
And puts his trust   in worthless dust   since all his wealth
    will come to naught.
Can't he recall?   Time swallows all,   including gold and
    man's high station.
Does he forget   the days that yet   will make him groan in
    tribulation?
All that remains   are endless pains   that no drug heals or
    sets aright;
The sun's last ray   then fades away,   revealing only
    endless night.
Then women mourners make their rounds   as huddled
    families grieve and moan:
"Mercy and forgiveness are the Lord's alone."

A further change in attitudes toward death is apparent in Western Europe in the centuries that followed. According to Ariès, the
old truth of *Et muriemur,* "we likewise [all] die," began to give way
to a new mentality, one that "reveals the importance, given through
the entire modern period, of the self to one's own existence, and
which can be expressed by another phrase, *la mort de soi,* 'one's own

death.'" Now, gradually, a person's death, no matter what the specific circumstances, took on "an anxious sense of nothingness, which finds no solace in hope of the beyond, although this hope continues to be expressed."[20] The theme of death's inevitability thus came to be replaced by the new, overwhelming realization that this particular individual was to disappear forever. The fact that other people's existence, indeed, the life of the deceased's own children and grandchildren, would go on without him was scant consolation, being overshadowed by the utter blackness of his own, individual cessation.

I have read quite a few studies that seek to date "the rise of the individual."[21] Depending on who you read, the individual first emerged in the second millennium BCE in Mesopotamia, or in late pre-exilic Israel; or no, in classical Greek civilization, I mean in imperial Rome, or make that: in Augustine's *Confessions,* with the rise of Islamic science, or else in twelfth-century Western Europe, the Italian Renaissance, the Protestant Reformation, with Descartes, no Leibniz, and so forth. On balance, it seems unwise to think of the emergence of our sense of self as a datable event in history, rather than a long process. Still, it seems undeniable that part of that process is mirrored in the changing attitudes toward death and dying chronicled by Ariès; his survey demonstrates that, starting in late medieval times, a greater orientation toward the individual and his or her ceasing-to-be did indeed begin to appear, and that things have continued to evolve in the same basic direction ever since.

The end point of Ariès's survey, death in contemporary England and America, highlights the bizarre reality in which we now live: death is virtually taboo.[21] People now die, for the most part, out of plain sight, in hospitals or hospices. Their bodies are then whisked away to funeral parlors and dressed up not in the shrouds of days gone by, but in their finest suit or dress, as if they were just about to step out and, hence, *not dead at all.* Or else—in fact, increasingly in America—their bodies are simply cremated, the ashes to be packaged in a convenient-sized urn and handed over to the dead person's survivors. No muss, no fuss.

✦ ✦ ✦

This is all part of humanity's great march up to the present. Even the one thing that we undeniably don't control—our own death—has gone from part of what God, or the Great Outside, used to do to each of us (since we were small human beings back then) to being the tragic end of a *big* human being's existence, to being something we would rather not confront openly, something we would prefer to move out of plain sight.

No one, least of all the present writer, can regret the material benefits that have accompanied this great march. Over the course of many centuries, we have come to understand more and more of the world, and with that understanding has come an infinitely greater measure of control over our own existence. Medicine, physics and chemistry, high-tech and biotech, agriculture and manufacturing—there is no end to cataloguing all the ways in which we have taken control of the elements that make up our existence. We long ago stopped being afraid of most things and we no longer scrutinize the world for signs.

I suppose the next sentence should start off, "But we have lost something in the process . . ." That is certainly true: so much of our apprehension of the divine used to focus on all that was beyond our control—rainfall and prosperity and lunar eclipses. As these things came to be explained scientifically and even predicted, the home base of our old apprehension of God began to evaporate and shrink, like a rain puddle in the bright sun. (This, of course, has nothing to do with the reality of God, but only with how humans had become accustomed to think about God.) Instead of pursuing this rather obvious point, however, I would rather focus on our modern selves and their present condition. Because surely *we* have changed in the process of acquiring all this knowledge; we are no longer the creatures we used to be. So I have to return to that crucial moment with which I began, sitting in the late-summer sun and being suddenly without the music, simply contained. It is hard, it is so, so hard, to resist filling what we see as the void all around us, filling it with those emanations that project out of our little beings off into space. Our modern denial of death, Ariès's book seeks to argue, is really a symptom of something larger, the way that we have come to conceive of "me myself." Death has become taboo in America because it spoils the myth of human control and our new, bigger selves.

Yet, when all is said and done, we still live the same pathetic handful of decades bemoaned by the author of Psalm 90: "The number of our days is seventy years, or if generously given, then eighty . . ." and this is the ultimate rebuke to our clumsy modern way of being. We may no longer be afraid of being eaten by tigers; we may know how to prevent all manner of diseases; in fact, we may understand so much nowadays that our world has lost almost all its capacity to frighten us with natural terrors (*almost* . . .). But we still do die, quite against our will—so what are we, really, big or small? Truly neither. We have outgrown our old, small selves, but our new, big ones have brought us to a rather unreal sense of the shape of our own existence, and in the bargain, we have lost what was most valuable, that old way of seeing—seeing ourselves and seeing the stark world that is just over there. The sociologist Max Weber (whose name, perhaps not coincidentally, means "weaver" in German) once observed that man is an animal suspended in webs of significance that he himself has spun, and such a view seems poignantly appropriate to modern man. There we hang, so big that we can barely see that which is real but altogether outside of ourselves, and utterly unable to return to what was an earlier, truer sense of things.

11

Medical Magic

Late in November, after three months of chemotherapy, I went (dragged myself) to a little retirement party arranged for a relative of mine, a gastroenterologist at the VA Hospital in Boston. I didn't have to go, but something told me it would be interesting to see a bunch of doctors (thirty or forty, as it turned out) in a setting in which I wasn't "the patient." My confidence that this would take place faltered slightly soon after I walked into the hall; several of the assembled, spotting my gray fuzz, immediately came up to me. "So, chemo," they said, rather matter-of-factly. "What have you got?" But their matter-of-factness made all the difference. Patients are used to a special sort of discourse with their doctors, and, consciously or not, doctors seem to encourage this. What they tell you is thus often spoken with a ponderousness bordering on the sententious—things like: "We can't cure your cancer, but we can certainly treat it." Only later does it occur to you that they must have uttered this sentence hundreds of times, to the point where it means almost nothing to them, save for its surefire palliative effect on the patient. Here, by contrast, the doctors were just among peers—the party was taking place in the hospital itself, and I'm pretty sure they all thought I was simply one of them, a specialist from some other ward (someone who, unfortunately but not uncommonly, was undergoing chemotherapy), rather than Eli's lone relative.

185

Which was what made the evening somewhat disturbing. One by one, they got up to say how much Eli would be missed. He was "the intellectual of the department," they said, "the philosopher," or even "the Talmud scholar." Listening to them go on, I couldn't help but agree. They didn't sound ignorant so much as totally unreflective, inhabitants of a narrow world of oft-repeated diagnoses and oft-prescribed therapies. It was, *mutatis mutandis,* like a gathering of automobile mechanics, people expert in telling you whether your fuel pump is shot or if you need a ring job, but whose out-of-the-garage diet of reading and reflection was likely to be either nothing at all or *Popular Mechanics.* Eli was different, they kept saying; he read and thought about things. Sometimes, they also said, he called into question the most basic things about what the hospital was doing or how they themselves were going about their jobs. Not everything he suggested got acted upon ("almost nothing," Eli told me later), but he did make everybody think, and that, they said, would surely (make that "sorely") be missed.

Why should they have been anything other than this? A doctor knows what he knows, and in our own age, his knowledge is increasingly specialized, which is to say narrow: he can treat ailments in certain parts of the body—which he does, day after day—but when it comes to other parts, he is altogether out of his depth; he performs certain procedures, but only them. Yet somehow we wish to maintain the illusion that doctors are just all-around smart—and not just about medicine. I remember once hearing a lecture given by a professor at one of the medical schools in the greater Boston area. His subject was something like "The Clinician's Calling," and part of that calling, he stressed, was to educate the patient about the nature of his or her illness. "In fact," he said, "that's why we're called *physicians:* 'physician' just means 'teacher' in Greek." Okay, I thought, so he's not very good at languages; he meant to say *doctor,* which indeed comes from the Latin verb that means "to teach" (although this title never meant "teacher" in the sense that he intended). But does this make him any less good at what he does? Still, I have to admit that

I would be a little reluctant to seek out the services of this man. He shattered the illusion.

The illusion is crucial. "Virtually all doctors," wrote the anthropologist Marcel Mauss in his classic study of magic in premodern societies, "are magicians. Their skills go hand in hand with magic, and in any case, their use of complex techniques makes it inevitable that their profession should be considered marvelous and supernatural."[1] This is true even today: if one had to look for some area of modern life that still preserves the faith and wonderment with which humans once approached magic, it would certainly be medicine. Most people still relate to doctors with an awe absent from other professionals. We may call our lawyers or accountants "Bob," but our doctors are still largely "Doctor." Schooled in a specialized lore that we could never hope to fathom, they are Men or Women of Knowledge, to whom we entrust our very lives—it can't get more serious than that. They treat us by prescribing substances that, for the most part, we have never heard of before and to which we ourselves have no access. These too have an inevitably magical quality: swallow this, insert that, and suddenly your life will be different. Even the instructions sound magical: "Take three times a day, allowing the capsule's contents to dissolve slowly under the tongue; do not swallow!"

To say this is not very complimentary to the medical profession; after all, what we call magic today is just a trick, the domain of illusionists and charlatans. What they do is arrange things in the room before you arrive—the specially marked deck of cards, the innocent-looking table draped with long black velvet, the mirror, the hat and gloves, the secret compartment—and then act as if you and they have just arrived at this place at the same time, as if nothing has been prepared. What fools we are to be taken in! But (as magicians themselves often point out), we really want to be taken in; otherwise we wouldn't be there. That is to say, our minds are moving in two opposite directions simultaneously: one part is looking for the obvious subterfuge while the other part is taking delight in not finding it. "Well, it looks like the laws of gravity, elementary physics, and simple logic have been broken!" the second part of us exults. "Maybe minds really can bend spoons." And it's interesting that this is not a disturbing thought. After all, most people want to live in an orderly, rule-following universe—shouldn't we be bothered by something that seems to break all the rules so flagrantly? But there's really nothing threatening about believing a parlor trick. It can't hurt *us,* and in the meanwhile, we may actually take comfort in the belief that not everything is understood, that not every phenomenon is susceptible to rational explanation.

Medicine, on the other hand, is not a trick; it's deadly serious. Yet doctors themselves know well that what they do functions a bit like magic; here too, we want to be taken in, we want to believe that whatever pills they prescribe or operation they perform will bring us complete relief. In fact, this belief can be crucial; numerous studies have shown that patients' mental state measurably affects their response to treatment. Doctors are well acquainted with the "placebo effect," whereby patients receiving an utterly ineffective, sham medication nevertheless sometimes show quantifiable improvements in their condition; true, the extent of this phenomenon has been debated back and forth, but the subject continues to receive the serious attention of researchers.[2] And it's not just *substances* that can change things; the very presence of the doctor can make things happen. How often does a patient say, "You know, I had this terrible pain until the minute I stepped into your office." On the other hand is the "white coat phenomenon," whereby patients' blood pressure actually goes up into the dangerous range simply by dint of its being measured by a nurse or a doctor; testing themselves at home, the same patients are far below the doctor's office reading.

With regard to my own treatment, I have mentioned chemotherapy, but that was only part of what the doctors prescribed for me. In fact, as soon as the cancer was discovered I was put on a special, experimental program (what doctors call a "protocol," since it usually involves outside funding that is granted on the basis of a treatment protocol submitted to the funder). This turned out to involve a whole range of things—"the kitchen sink approach," one of the doctors said: surgery, chemotherapy, radiation, drugs. Each of these works on the patient's body in different ways; no doubt such a combination also has some effect on the mind, though it's always hard to say anything more than that—and in any case, the "mind" part is not on any protocol that I've ever heard of. In fact, it's rather curious, and not a little ironic, that part of the magic of our own modern medicine rests on our denial of the "mind" part of being healed. We like to believe that modern medicine simply overwhelms disease (not only in the patient, but in the abstract), so that the same procedures will have the same effects whether performed on optimist or pessimist, the medical skeptic or the true believer: cures belong to the immutable laws of science.

Along with this goes a rather snobbish view of "our" medicine as the only real kind, the culmination of decades of scientific research, whereas anything else is voodoo. This we believe with a perfect faith—which is also ironic, since, however wrongheaded, it probably helps our minds to think that we are getting the only real sort of treatment available, and hence, to be made whole again. Some Americans may still remember the time when James Reston, a well-known *New York Times* correspondent, was suddenly stricken with appendicitis during a visit to China. He was rushed to the hospital, where part of his postoperative treatment included acupuncture. Acupuncture was virtually unknown in the United States at the time, and the headline of the article that Reston wrote about his experience expressed his utter amazement: "I've seen the past and it works!" Almost single-handedly, this article turned acupuncture into a serious form of treatment in America, even (here's the American acid test!) a reimbursable one. Nevertheless, our minds still largely think about disease and treatment in the most rigidly Western, modern sort of way.

✦ ✦ ✦

The surgeon Richard Seltzer, who has written with great insight and sensitivity about his profession, describes in one of his books the visit to his New Haven hospital of a certain Yeshi Dhonden, "Personal Physician to the Dalai Lama." The Tibetan doctor had come, apparently, to swap medical pointers with his Western colleagues, though at first his appearance—"a short, golden, barrelly man dressed in a sleeveless robe of saffron and maroon; his scalp is shaven, and the only visible hair is a scanty black line above each hooded eyebrow"— hardly identified him as a member of the same guild as Seltzer's New Haven colleagues.

The doctors had decided to ask Yeshi Dhonden to examine a severely ill patient without, however, informing him of her symptoms or their diagnosis.

The patient had been awakened early and told that she was to be examined by a foreign doctor, and had been asked to produce a fresh specimen of urine, so when we enter her room, the woman shows no surprise. She has long ago taken on that mixture of compliance and resignation that is the facies of chronic illness. This was to be but another in an endless series of tests and examinations. Yeshi Dhonden steps to the bedside while the rest [of us] stand apart, watching. For a long time he gazes at the woman, favoring no part of her body with his eyes, but seeming to fix his glance at a place just above her supine form. I, too, study her. No physical sign nor obvious symptom gives a clue as to the nature of her disease.

At last he takes her hand, raising it in both of his own. Now he bends over the bed in a kind of crouching stance, his head drawn down into the collar of his robe. His eyes are closed as he feels for her pulse. In a moment he has found the spot, and for the next half hour he remains thus, suspended above the patient like some exotic golden bird with folded wings, holding the pulse of the woman beneath his fingers, cradling her hand in his . . .

At last Yeshi Dhonden straightens, gently places the woman's hand upon the bed, and steps back. His interpreter produces a small wooden bowl and two sticks. Yeshi Dhonden pours a portion of the urine specimen into the bowl, and proceeds to whip the liquid with the two sticks. This he does for several minutes until a foam is raised. Then, bowing above the bowl, he inhales the odor three times. He sets down the bowl and turns to leave. All this while, he has not uttered a single word. As he nears the door, the woman raises her head and calls out to him in a voice at once urgent and serene. "Thank you, doctor," she says, and touches with her other hand the place he had held on her wrist, as though to recapture something that had visited there.

Later, the doctors convene in a conference room to hear what the Tibetan visitor, speaking through the interpreter, has to say about what he has seen.

He speaks of winds coursing through the body of the woman, currents that break against barriers, eddying. These vortices are in her blood, he says. The last spending of an imperfect heart. Between the chambers of her heart, long, long before she was born, a wind had come and blown open a deep gate that must never be opened. Through it charge the full waters of her river, as the mountain stream cascades in the springtime, battering, knocking loose the land, and flooding her breath. Thus he speaks, and is silent.

"May we have the [hospital's] diagnosis?" a professor asks.

The host of these rounds, the man who knows, answers.

"Congenital heart disease," he says. "Interventricular septal defect, with resultant heart failure."

A gateway in the heart, I think. That must not be opened. Through it charge the full waters that flood her breath. So! Here then is the doctor listening to the sounds of the body to which the rest of us are deaf. He is more than doctor. He is priest.[3]

✦ ✦ ✦

A priest indeed. People forget that this was true of the world of the Bible as well. Part of the ancient Israelite priest's job was to diagnose various skin diseases—rashes, swellings, discolorations on the face or body, and in particular an affliction known as *tsara'at* (unfortunately mistranslated as "leprosy" by the early Greek translators of the Pentateuch; its actual nature is now unknown). The priests were the ones to tell you if your *tsara'at* was still contagious, as well as how to banish it from your hair, beard, clothes, or the stones of your house. Then, after you had been healed, you had to be *cleansed* by the priest, and here, too, certain specific steps had to be followed. Even in a society that officially banned magicians, wizards, mediums, and the like, what the priest did sounds very much like magic to modern ears:

> The priest shall command that two live, ritually pure birds, and some cedar wood, crimson cloth and hyssop, be brought for the one who is to be cleansed. The priest shall command that one of the birds be slaughtered over fresh water in an earthen vessel. He shall then take the living bird, along with the cedar wood and the crimson cloth and the hyssop, and dip them and the living bird into the blood of the bird that was slaughtered over the fresh water. He shall then sprinkle it [the blood] seven times upon the one who is to be cleansed of the eruption and pronounce him clean; then he shall let the living bird fly off into the open country. (Leviticus 14:4–7)

After decades of trying to pin down the difference between magic and religion, many scholars have become convinced that there really isn't any: we readily identify as magic something in someone else's religion, but we see quite similar things in our own as simply what we do, a rite or sacrament or ancient custom. This observation is, of course, disturbing to people who take their own religion seriously; as already noted, magic nowadays is a trick or an illusion, practiced by those who claim (even in magic's modern, debased sense) to have special powers. No doubt there was a good deal of that in ancient magic/religion as well. Religion is, as I have been trying to argue, a kind of openness: its openness to charlatans and superstition simply comes with the territory, comes with its *fundamental* openness to that which cannot be seen by the eyes or heard by the ears. But even the American who thinks himself altogether beyond all that is nevertheless open to being cured by modern medicine; as usual, the strongest beliefs are the ones of which we are unaware.

The matter of what exactly cures us is not unrelated to other themes that have run through this book, in particular that of the semipermeable soul and "who shall I say is calling?" After all, if "I" am on the inside, really me, why can't *I* get those little cancer cells to stop reproducing? Or is there some apparently outside *I* who, like the God of old, needs to be summoned, persuaded to cross the curtain? An e-mail I got a few weeks ago from a friend suffering from stage III breast cancer:

> I continue to do well, still having treatment, but not feeling too battered by it and most importantly my condition does not seem to be worsening in any significant way. It certainly is a challenge to live with uncertainty, embrace it even, and to relate to my body as an environment that I need to make compatible and conducive to life. Tai Chi, meditation, veganism, and *tefillah* all help.

The last sentence intrigued me. Tai Chi (at least as practiced in many places now) is a set of gentle, dancelike movements, "meditation in motion," designed to reduce stress and promote a feeling of well-being. It is thus a physical activity aimed at, among other things, creating results in the mind. Meditation, it would be fair to say, is a similar combination of the physical and the mental performed toward the same end. Veganism, a strict form of vegetarianism, is a diet designed to promote health and effect cures. All these, in other words, are presumably aimed at getting my friend's "inside" into better shape to fight the cancer. But how does *tefillah* (the Hebrew word for prayer), fit in with these three? My friend didn't say.

Some people today, even though they are religious, tend to regard prayer as another form of meditation or relaxation. It's not really *intended* to produce results, they say, and so it doesn't really matter if there's Anyone listening on the other end; it's all about getting in touch with your inner self. Personally, I think this is all wrong; there has to be something at stake, something *real* going on. And the real thing that's going on has to be somewhere in the human brain and in the posture of reaching out from that brain to what is entirely outside of itself. If that reaching out has no reality, I don't see the point. It's not exactly analogous, but I remember what the devout Catholic writer Flannery O'Connor once wrote about the Eucharist: "If it's a symbol, the hell with it."

In biblical times, if the Bible itself is an accurate representation, people did not pray all that much—and certainly not in order to get in touch with their inner selves. True, in the thick of things, they might sometimes cry out to God. "Save me from my brother Esau," Jacob prays, thinking Esau is coming to kill him, and, "O God! Heal her now!" Moses prays after his sister, Miriam, has been stricken. But generally their principal way of "speaking" with God was through the offering of animal sacrifices in the temple. Bulls, goats, lambs, and birds were slaughtered and offered on the altar in the temple. Commonly, people in crisis would make vows to offer such a sacrifice: heal me now and I'll pay up later. And they would pay up, dragging their sheep or goat to the temple in order to be slaughtered and sacrificed, and so complete the transaction. (Failure to honor the vow was sure to bring down divine punishment.) Sacrificing animals was hardly a unique feature of Israel's religion; all over the ancient Near East (and well beyond its borders), such offerings were thought to be the appropriate way for people to communicate with the deity. It's not that the idea of prayer didn't occur to them, it just didn't seem to carry much weight on its own. As Platonis Sallustius, a fourth-century philosopher and author of *On the Gods and the World* observed, "Prayer without sacrifice is just words." God, who is "out there," required something more than our well-intended speech.

What people thought they were doing by slaughtering an animal and hoisting it onto an altar is far from clear. Like many other things (including prayer as well), the people doing it did not necessarily reflect on why they were doing it. Among the various reasons that have been proposed by scholars: (1) the sacrifice was conceived as the deity's food (gods presumably need to eat, and the animal flesh, vaporized on the altar, could then be consumed by the deity); (2) the sacrifice was a substitute for the sacrificer's own life (that is, "Take this animal in place of me"); (3) the sacrifice was something precious, part of one's personal wealth, so that giving it to the god was a sign of one's fealty and utter devotion to him or her (this is presumably part of what Sallustius was getting at—money talks louder than words); (4) the sacrifice was essentially the food of a communal feast uniting the worshiper with the deity.[4]

Of course, *what* people sacrificed obviously has some bearing on why they did it, and here the evidence is somewhat surprising; sacrifices went well beyond domestic animals or birds. In fact, over much of the ancient world, in North and South America, Europe, the Near East, India, and elsewhere, there is good evidence that people sometimes sacrificed other people. The sacrificial victim could be a member of the sacrificer's own family—a beloved son, for example[5]—or a household slave or someone captured in war. No matter who it was, this practice is horrifying to modern sensibilities; it does, however, attest to the seriousness of sacrificing. Someone who offered the life of his own son to a god wasn't performing some bland ritual, but giving up all that was dearest to himself, and offering it to a god who, presumably, would not be spurred to action by anything less. The Bible recounts that King Mesha, the ninth-century ruler of neighboring Moab, went to war against the combined forces of Israel, Judah, and Edom. Mesha was losing badly when he undertook a desperate move:

When the King of Moab saw that the battle was going against him, he took with him seven hundred swordsmen to break through, opposite the king of Edom; but he could not. Then he took his firstborn son who was to succeed him and offered him as burnt offering on the wall. And great wrath came upon Israel, so they withdrew from [attacking] him and returned to their own land. (2 Kings 3:26–27)

Apparently, Mesha's killing his own son did the trick.

Sometimes people also sacrificed their own blood or their own limbs. Psalm 137 reports that when the people of Judah were conquered by the Babylonians, many of them were brought as captives back to Babylon itself—including the musicians (presumably temple musicians) who apparently wrote this psalm. Once in Babylon, their guards demanded that they sing and play for them, but the captive Judeans refused:

There [in Babylon] we hung up our lyres on poplar trees,
since our captors had demanded that we sing, and our
        tormentors [demanded] celebration, "Sing us one of
        those Zion songs!"
How can we sing a song of the LORD on foreign soil?

These verses puzzled ancient biblical interpreters. How could the captives refuse a direct order from the Babylonians, hanging up their instruments in a symbolic gesture of defiant refusal? Weren't the Babylonians in a position to *make* them sing, by force if necessary? One interpretation therefore suggested that, at the very moment the Babylonians made this demand, all the lyre players simultaneously bit off their fingers; then, showing the bloody stumps to their captors, they asked, "*How* can we sing a song of the LORD on foreign soil?"[6]

This always seemed to me a highly imaginative way of explaining the psalm, until I read Walter Burkert's account of finger sacrifice in ancient Greece; such a thing was apparently not uncommon:

Near Megalopolis in Arcadia, Pausanias records, there was a sanctuary of the Furies . . . with a small mound nearby called the Finger Memorial (*Dactulou Mnema*) . . . The story goes that Orestes,
having killed his mother, was driven mad by the Furies just there,
until he bit off one of his fingers . . . This ritual was probably still
performed at the sanctuary during Pausanias' lifetime. Pursuing
demons are pacified by the act of severing a finger from the body;
the partial loss is to save the whole man.[7]

Nor was this form of sacrifice exclusive to the Hellenic world.
Burkert cites Sir James Frazer who, in characteristically broad
strokes, had surveyed finger sacrifice throughout the world:

In Tonga on the Friendly Islands it was common practice to cut off
a finger or portion of one as a sacrifice to the gods for the recovery
of a superior relative who was sick; earlier, Captain Cook reported
the same thing: "They suppose that the devil will accept the little finger as a sort of sacrifice efficacious enough to procure the
recovery of their health." Likewise, "Hottentot women and Bush-
women cut off a joint of a child's finger, especially if a previous
child has died. The sacrifice of the finger joint is supposed to save
the second child's life . . ." "Among the Blackfeet, in times of great
public or private necessity, a warrior cuts off a finger of his left
hand and offers it to the Morning Star at its rising."[8]

But here is the point: Whatever these people *thought* they were
doing, it surely did not always work. Plenty of times, no doubt,
they would sacrifice their precious animals, their fingers, their
own children, and then . . . Nothing. The sick person would die,
the battle would be lost, their land would be conquered. At some
point someone must undoubtedly have said: "This just isn't effec-
tive. Whatever the gods want, they don't want these sacrifices!"
But if there ever was such a person, no one listened to him, because
in the end that wasn't what it was all about. As Godfrey Lien-

hardt observed about the Dinka: "They do not expect sacrifice automatically to achieve some specific result with the certainty of a well-tested technical procedure." Which brings us back to the button-pushing professors and the need to do something and "Man proposes, and God disposes." In other words, what the sacrificers did was to take what was most dear to them and, in losing it, enact a relationship, a bloody, fearsome enacting of how they fit into the world—perhaps, one might even say, of their being no more than themselves, looking outward and upward in the desperate dignity of their smallness.

When the treatment is all finished, all you can do is wait. I remember very clearly that for months afterwards, I felt like a ghost—at times invisible and at other times just semivisible, like the ghosts of George and Marion who haunted Cosmo Topper in the popular TV show of my youth. For quite a long time I really wasn't ready to commit myself mentally to being anything but "in transition," on my way from something known to something yet to be decided.

I remember thinking often in those days about someone I had known twenty years earlier, when I was a young professor at Yale. He was older, a law professor in his forties, who lived a block from us in New Haven. We were never particularly close, but he and his wife had been kind enough to invite my family over when we first arrived, and I would sometimes ride with him on the bus that took us past Edgewood Park to the university campus. Then he got brain cancer; one day, he just lost sensation in the fingers of both hands. A friend of his wife later told me that he suspected what it was right away; he and his wife then began running "from pillar to post" (I remember the expression because it was the first time I had heard it) in an attempt to find some new treatment or experimental drug that might help. Before all this, he had once spoken expansively with me about his future plans as a scholar—there was to be some book, an encyclopedia of some sort, that he wanted to write or perhaps edit, something that he hoped would change the whole way that people thought about the relationship of law and morality.

He did get some kind of treatment, though I'm not sure what it was. What I do remember is seeing him back at the bus stop one spring morning, one of those mornings when the buds are first appearing on the spindly, greenish, purplish shoots sprouting out of elm boughs and a kind of moist, muddy smell comes rising up out of people's lawns. He looked completely grotesque—head shaven and scarred, pale, thinner by at least ten pounds, swimming in a light-colored summer suit, and holding a heavy leather briefcase. It was clear he just wanted me to treat him like his old self and talk as we usually did, but I could hardly look at him. I think it was only a few months later that he died. Talking to a neighbor a week or so after the funeral, I learned another new expression. We were discussing declining real estate values and the middle-class exodus from our part of town. Gesturing with her chin toward the dead law professor's house, she said, "That's the only way I'll ever leave my place— feetfirst, like him."

I suppose that, when I had completed the whole treatment, I was no easier to look at than he was that day at the bus stop: hairless, thin, tired. "Feetfirst" was still an altogether vivid possibility in my mind. But one day, in that blurry, post-chemotherapy daze, when I was still walking around the house in my pajamas, the phone rang. The woman on the other end was telling me that one of my books had just won a prestigious prize, one that carried a very big monetary award, in fact, more money than any other book prize I had ever heard of. ("Your uncle in Australia has died and you are pope.") She and the other people in the prize-granting organization of course knew nothing about my having cancer, so she was rather nonchalant as she read off the conditions that were attached to the prize. I was to fly down to Louisville for the awards ceremony, to which my wife was also invited, and, apparently for tax reasons, the prize money was to be awarded in equal installments over a period of five years. "If, for some reason," she added without even a nervous laugh, "the prize recipient should die before the five-year period is over, the remaining payments will be forfeited."

I hung up the phone with a mixture of excitement and anxiety. Would I make it through the next five years? There was no reason to think so. But by the time the ceremony in Louisville took place, I somehow felt certain I would, though I'm still not sure why.

12

Postscript

Two and a half years have passed since I started writing this book, ten years since I got sick. I still go in for regular checkups. This past year, I was invited to be a visiting professor at a university in New York City. An old classmate, now an important New York lawyer, fixed me up with his own doctor for the year—"the best diagnostician in New York." I had my medical records forwarded to him, and he ran me through an extremely thorough battery of tests, which lasted for two days. Later, he phoned me with the results.

"You need to start taking some vitamin D, you're way low on that. And your cholesterol's a little high. But the good news is, the cancer isn't back."

"Good news? You make it sound as if it *could* be back."

"Well, you never know."

"But that was nine years ago. Isn't there some sort of statute of limitations?"

"I suppose every year cancer-free is a plus. But I've been over your records pretty carefully. To tell you the truth, I don't know why you got better."

"But the protocol they put me on . . ."

"Oh, that! I'm sure it helped. But your doctors published an article about it a couple years after you went on it. It turns out the results really weren't any better than with conventional therapies. No, I don't know. The important thing is that you feel okay now. And that you keep going in for checkups every six months or so."

"Well, if it wasn't the protocol, then why did I get better?"

"I couldn't say for sure. There are some cancers that just go away. No one knows why."

Teiresias is a figure from ancient Greek folklore, the archetypal sage. His wisdom, according to legend, came to him as a result of a particular happening. One day he was out walking in the forest and stepped on a pair of copulating snakes. It is not clear if this was deliberate or accidental, but whichever the case, Teiresias was immediately punished by being transformed into a woman. For seven years he walked about as a female, until he again came upon the snakes and was thereupon turned back into a man. Once restored to his former state, he became the wisest man in Greece.

One day in the hospital, on my way to chemotherapy, I stepped by accident on a hospital brochure that had fallen to the floor. Lifting up my foot, I noticed the symmetrical twin snakes curling around a sword (the traditional caduceus of the brochure's logo), and the thought suddenly occurred to me that after this, if I survived, nothing would ever be the same. But it turns out I was wrong. Things have pretty much returned to what they were before. I still teach my classes and I still write books and articles about the Bible and the Dead Sea Scrolls. It's only every once in a while that I have a flash of memory. Then, for a minute, I do feel a little like Teiresias, as if everything is really very clear, and my heart is full of love for this earthly existence.

As for today's neuroscientists and evolutionary biologists who study the origins of religion, I certainly have no argument with them about either scientific methods or their goal. We work for the same employer, after all, and share many of the same assumptions. But I think they have misunderstood the most fundamental element of religious belief. It is not God's sovereignty over the entire universe that is at issue so much as His sovereignty over the cubic centimeter of space that sits just in front of our own noses. That is to say, religion is first of all about fitting into the world and fitting into one's borders. There may indeed be something "mythic" about it, but it pales before the mythic quality of our own clumsy, modern selves. Here we are, living on a tiny speck of a planet on the outskirts of a cosmic explosion, but that meeting next Thursday afternoon is *so* important. Why it is important is wrapped up in the supreme myth that we unwittingly inhabit, whose origins are indeed connected to all the things that evolutionary biologists and neuroscientists study (though of course, their research hasn't noted the extent to which we have carried these ancient instincts into wholly new, and rather bizarre, configurations in our own age). But these myths of ours are quite pointless in a moment of privileged insight, when we are enabled to catch a glimpse of what lies beyond our own real being. Such a moment may come at any time, but it is, as I have been trying to argue, the foundation on which the religious consciousness is built—though sometimes, I admit, it takes a doctor's diagnosis or a verdict of death to bring it into focus. Then we can hear, as for the first time, the same words that Boethius heard: "Turn yourselves away from vice and practice virtue; lift your minds up to proper hopes, and offer up humble prayers to Heaven. A great necessity is imposed upon you (if you don't hide from the truth): to do what is right, since whatever you do is done in the sight of a Judge who sees all things."

And also this: Why is it that the gods of different nations are so often said to live "in heaven"? One might suppose the reason is that heaven is the remotest spot we can name; if they lived anywhere closer, it might not be easy to explain why we don't run into them on a daily basis. But in truth, that's not the reason for their heavenly abode. After all, some classical deities were indeed said to live down here: they dwelt in the ground beneath people's feet, or in the ocean, in the winds, or were thought to be immanent in this tree, this rock, or this man-made statue. No, it seems that the heavenly gods are up there, at least in part, because of heaven's perspective: it is from on high that the gods can look down and see all of human life, and so see us in our full smallness. For the same reason, all along the eastern Mediterranean and beyond, temples were built on mountaintops, since mountaintops are at least halfway to heaven. Up there, gods and men could meet: the men could climb up to placate the gods and the gods could come down to be placated, without, however, losing their heavenly purchase on everything going on down below. Olympus, the highest mountain in Greece, housed twelve gods and goddesses; Canaanite El inhabited Mount Saphon (Jabl al-Aqra'); and Israel's God lived on Sinai, "the mountain of God/the gods." Sometimes, ancient peoples even built an artificial mountain, like the Babylonian ziggurat, to simulate ascent. (I remember the unironic title of a conference paper I once heard, "The Theme of the Sacred Mountain at Ugarit and in the Hebrew Bible: An Overview of Recent Scholarship.") Climbing up, the humans inevitably gained something of the gods' perspective on themselves. "I've been to the mountaintop," said Martin Luther King the day before he was killed.

I have visited ancient temples, but truthfully, my own lofty sanctuary is the place in which I often find myself nowadays (in fact, where I am right now, writing these lines), high above the earth in a sturdy Boeing aircraft. I fly to some scholarly conference and then fly back again, watching the late-afternoon sun as it sinks—too fast or too slow, depending on the plane's direction—into the horizon.

> What do you think has become of the young and old men?
> And what do you think has become of the women and children?
> They are alive and well somewhere;
> The smallest sprout shows there is really no death;
> And if ever there was, it led forward life, and does not wait at the
> end to arrest it,
> And ceas'd the moment life appear'd. (Walt Whitman, *Leaves of Grass*)

In the two and a half years that I have been writing this book, I have lost a few friends to cancer; their names are written at the front of the volume. None of them was particularly young, but none was particularly old, either. What does it matter if God, or a defective gene somewhere, chose to slice off a decade or two from their expected lifetimes? Certainly not much when one is 30,000 feet above the earth. Down there, of course, we cling to life, trying to squeeze every last minute out of it, and rightly so: it's all we've got. Yet somehow we never quite manage to lose the mountaintop perspective, that is, the secret life of starkness in our brains; so we maintain a ghostly dialogue with what is not at all our down-there selves. This dialogue has absolutely no survival value, but we can't stop it. As a result, it's always going, whether we're aware of it or not; and when, for a moment, we are aware, we know it speaks the truth.

I remember one of those friends recently dead, who had cancer of the esophagus—the radiation so blasted out his saliva glands that afterwards, everywhere he went he carried a bottle of Neviyot water with him, drinking from it cheerfully at 20-second intervals for nearly two years. The last time I saw him in the hospital he ignored us, his friends, in favor of a soccer match on TV, getting up out of his chair from time to time, as if suddenly remembering something, then sitting down again. He died the next day.

She . . . one day on a walk near the Potomac, she kept yelling the names of her two dogs, who had taken off unexpectedly on their own; she got hoarser and hoarser—as if *they* were the ones in danger. She knew the truth, of course. The only time I ever saw her cry (I knew her for exactly forty years, from the time she was 18) was a few weeks after her diagnosis, when I asked if she had told her sons. She just burst into tears. Well, of course! That's the life down there. But during her last week of life, she drifted in and out of a coma, ascending in jerky, Z-like motions toward the top of the mountain. From way up here, I can see her, I can see you all, floating.
Sincerely, J. Kugel

Acknowledgments

I wish to express my thanks to the Oxford Centre for Hebrew and Jewish Studies (Yarnton Manor) and to the Tikvah Center at New York University, under whose auspices I wrote some sections of this book. It would be too long to thank all those individuals who have contributed in one way or another to the completion of this project, so I will instead limit myself to mentioning a single name, that of Mary Ellen Morrissey, whose help has been deeply appreciated.

Notes

2. MAN STANDS POWERLESS
BEFORE ELEVATOR

1. Actually, "God is the bigger" is a still more literal translation—and not an insignificant detail for my overall theme. I should also point out that in Arabic, the form *akbar* alone is ambiguous: it can be either the comparative or the superlative form of the adjective, hence the common translation "God is the greatest."

2. Berger continues: This leads to the consequence that the individual's own biographical misfortunes, including the final misfortune of having to die, are weakened at least in their anomic impact by being apprehended as only episodes in the continuing history of the collectivity with which the individual is identified. The stronger this identification, the weaker will be the threat of anomy arising from the misfortunes of individual biography. To be sure, there still remains a problem of legitimating certain collective misfortunes, such as epidemics, or famines, or foreign conquests, and specific theodicies may be established for this purpose. This task is, however, made easier by the identification of the individual with his collectivity for a very simple reason: the individual's mortality is empirically available, while that of the collectivity, typically, is not. The individual knows that he will die and, consequently, that some of his misfortunes can never be alleviated within his lifetime. If he loses a limb, for instance, it can never be restored to him. The collectivity, on the other hand, can usually be conceived of as immortal. It may suffer misfortunes, but these can be interpreted as only transitory episodes in its overall history. Thus the individual dying on the battlefield at the hands of the foreign conqueror may not look forward to his own resurrection or immortality, but he can do so with regard to his group. To the extent that he subjectively identi-

fies himself with that group, his death will have meaning for him even if it is unembellished with any 'individualized' legitimations. Such identification, therefore, posits an implicit theodicy, without the need for further theoretical rationalization." See Peter L. Berger, *The Sacred Canopy: Elements of a Sociological Theory of Religion* (Garden City, N. Y.: Doubleday Anchor, 1976), 60–61. It is not altogether evident from this passage, but such an outlook is, in Berger's view, somewhat primitive; elsewhere he calls it "irrational." But this seems hardly fair. To view the world through the notion of self described by Berger is no more rational or irrational than to view the world in any other way. Indeed, the ability of this "identification of the individual with his collectivity" to cushion people from life's shocks and misfortunes would suggest that it may have much to recommend it.

3. Ryszard Kapuszinski, *The Shadow of the Sun* (New York: Vintage, 2002), 36–37.

4. Claude Lévi-Strauss, *Tristes tropiques,* trans. J. and D. Weightman (New York: Penguin Books, 1992), 234.

5. Hazel R. Markus and S. Kitayama, "Cultural Variation in the Self-Concept," in Jaine Strauss and G. R. Goethals, *The Self: Interdisciplinary Approaches* (Berlin: Springer Verlag, 1991), 18–48; see also D. Kondo, "Work, family and the self: A Cultural analysis of Japanese family enterprise," Ph.D. diss., Harvard, 1982, and T. S. Lebra, *Japanese Patterns of Behavior* (Honolulu: University of Hawaii Press, 1976).

6. See on this M. Bayliss, "The Cult of Dead Kin in Assyria and Babylonia," *Iraq* 35 (1973), 115–25; Brian B. Schmidt, *Israel's Beneficent Dead: Ancestor Cult and Necromancy in Ancient Israelite Religion and Tradition* (Winona Lake, Ind.: Eisenbrauns, 1996), 201–15; Theodore Lewis, *The Cult of the Dead in Ancient Israel and Ugarit* (Atlanta: Scholars Press, 1989), 97.

3. HOPE

1. Randall Jarrell, *The Complete Poems* (New York: Farrar, Straus and Giroux, 1969).

4. RELIGION ON THE BRAIN

1. See on these the general survey of E. E. Evans-Pritchard, *Theories of Primitive Religion* (Oxford: Clarendon Press, 1965).

2. Such ideas were already being questioned in the nineteenth century, but they have shown remarkable staying power among run-of-the-mill debunkers of religion. They have also recently resurfaced in somewhat more sophisticated form. Religions are all remarkably violent, this new argument goes: they all seem to thrive on blood rites and animal sacrifices, because their original purpose was to defuse the inherently violent tendencies in humanity and channel them into relatively harmless ceremonies. This approach, associated primarily with René Girard and Walter Burkert, has lately been justly criticized; see J. Klawans, *Purity, Sacrifice, and the Temple: Symbolism and Supersessionism in the Study of Ancient Judaism* (New York: Oxford, 2006), 22–27.

3. This work has proceeded in various quarters under different names and with somewhat different foci. Thus, for a theoretical presentation and brief history of "human behavioral ecology": William Irons and Lee Cronk, "Two Decades of a New Paradigm," in Cronk et al., *Adaptation and Human Behavior: An Anthropological Perspective* (New York: De Gruyter, 2000). On "coevolution": W. H. Durham, *Coevolution: Genes, Culture, and Human Diversity* (Stanford, Calif.: Stanford University Press, 1991; cf. E. O. Wilson, *Sociobiology: The New Synthesis* (Cambridge, Mass.: Harvard University Press, 1975) and *idem, On Human Nature* (Cambridge, Mass.: Harvard University Press, 1978), and *Consilience: The Unity of Knowledge* (New York: Alfred A. Knopf, 1998).

4. The former term (a bit more accurate, it seems) is that of Scott Atran, *In Gods We Trust: the Evolutionary Landscape of Religion* (New York: Oxford University Press, 2002), 69. The latter was coined earlier by Justin Barrett and made popular by Richard Dawkins, Daniel Dennett, and others; see Dawkins, *The God Delusion* (New York: Houghton Mifflin, 2006), 213–14, and Dennett, *Breaking the Spell: Religion as a Natural Phenomenon* (New York: Penguin Books, 2006), 108–15.

5. This is connected to the phenomenon known to experimental psychologists as "theory of mind" (the term was apparently introduced by D. Premack and G. Woodruff, "Does the Chimpanzee Have a Theory of Mind?" *Behavioral and Brain Sciences* 4 [1978], 515–26). The phrase is now widely used as shorthand for our ability to attribute mental states—such as intentions, beliefs, and desires—to ourselves and to others, and to interpret, predict, and explain behavior in terms of mental states. Experiments have explored the phenomenon with children via the "Smarties task": Children are shown a box that looks as if it contains candy. The box is then opened and instead it turns out to contain pencils. The box is closed again, and the children are asked what other children, who haven't seen

inside the box, will think it contains. The average 4-year-old will answer that they will think it contains candy, whereas younger children answer pencils. This demonstrates that "very young children are unable to comprehend that other persons might have false beliefs." See D. Zahavi, "The Embodied Self-Awareness of the Infant," in D. Zahavi, Th. Gruenbaum, et al., *The Structure and Development of Self-Consciousness: Interdisciplinary Perspectives* (Amsterdam: John Benjamins, 2004), 38–39; also: M. Lewis and J. Brooks-Gunn, *Social Cognition and the Acquisition of Self* (New York: Plenum, 1979); M. Jeannerod, "From Self-Recognition to Self-Consciousness," in Zahavi et al., *Structure and Development,* 65–87.

6. See the discussion in Atran, *In Gods We Trust,* 43–45.

7. The idea of such an unintended switch goes back to Darwin's original description of evolution, but the term "exaptation" was first proposed by S. J. Gould and Elisabeth Vrba, "Exaptation—a missing term in the science of form," *Paleobiology* 8 (1982), 4–15.

8. In general: Steven Pinker, *The Blank Slate: The Modern Denial of Human Nature* (New York: Penguin Books, 2002).

9. This is not to say, of course, that moving an item from the very end of a sentence to its head never happens. Consider this sentence: "The very last thing I would call that glutinous mess they served for desert is *tempting.*" This can certainly be turned into *"Tempting* is the very last thing I would call that glutinous mess they served for desert." Yet even this is not simply a mechanical transfer of what otherwise would be the last word to the head of the sentence, since the "is" has to move as well. In other words, we are still dealing with grammatical categories and not merely random words; in this case, all that has happened is that the very long, complex subject has been moved from before to after the copula.

10. Steven Pinker, *The Language Instinct* (New York: HarperCollins Perennial, 2000), 29–30, 321.

11. P. Ekman et al., "Pan-Cultural Elements in Facial Displays of Emotion," *Science* 164 (1969), 86–88; *idem,* "Universals and Cultural Differences in Facial Expressions of Emotion," in J. K. Cole, *Nebraska Symposium on Motivation* (Lincoln: University of Nebraska Press, 1972), 207–83; Carroll E. Izard, *The Face of Emotion* (New York: Appleton-Century-Crofts, 1971); I. Eibl-Eibesfeldt, *Human Ethology* (New York: de Gruyter, 1989).

12. B. Berlin and Paul Kay, *Basic Color Terms: Their Universality and Evolution* (Berkeley: University of California Press, 1969).

13. Subsequent research has both refined the results of Berlin and Kay's study and enhanced our understanding of the underlying science. As one scholar (and, incidentally, a participant in the original study by Ber-

lin and Kay) has put it: "Regularities in the linguistic encoding of color result from regularities in the neural coding of color in the brain," W. H. Durham, *Coevolution: Genes, Culture, and Human Diversity* (Stanford, Calif.: Stanford University Press, 1991), 218. In other words, it is the way our brains are set up to process colors that has determined the colors we see and, consequently, why we tend to distinguish colors in similar ways (despite the surface diversity) in different human languages. The task of distinguishing color begins with the retina in our eyes—in the famous "rods and cones" that capture light and convert it into nerve-impulse energy. Our retinas contain three types of cones, each of which is maximally sensitive to either long wavelength ranges of light, medium wavelength ranges, or short wavelength ranges. (To be precise, experiments have shown that these cones do not react *exclusively* to a single wavelength range. They are actually stimulated by *any* light rays within the human visible range, but are more stimulated by one type of wavelength than the other two.) This is the physiological basis for what is called "trichromacy," that is, the three-color basis for human color vision. But the retinal stage is only the beginning. A special category of nerve cell, located at what is called the brain's "lateral geniculate nucleus" (LGN) in the thalamus, then compares the levels of activation in the retinal cones and further refines their input. There are actually four types of nerve cells involved: one responds positively to red and negatively to green; a second responds positively to green and negatively to red; a third responds positively to yellow and negatively to blue; while the fourth responds positively to blue and negatively to yellow. The fact that these nerve cells are polarized (that is, yes to red and, simultaneously, no to green; yes to yellow and no to blue; and so forth) suggests that this is why our languages do not have intermediate categories like "reddish-green" or "bluish-yellow." Finally, the visual cortex is where the last stage of neural coding takes place. There, the wavelength information passed on by the LGN cells is integrated into a coherent visual image that contains information about the hue, brightness, and color saturation (i.e., the relative purity of a color) of the perceived object. See on this Durham, *Coevolution,* 216–21.

14. See Donald E. Brown, *Human Universals* (New York: McGraw-Hill, 1991) and the list of universals based on it and published in Pinker, *The Blank Slate,* 435–39; also, Brown, "Human Universals and Their Implications," in N. Roughley, ed., *Being Humans: Anthropological Universality and Particularity in Transdisciplinary Perspectives* (New York: Walter de Gruyter, 2000).
15. Cf. Maimonides, *Mishneh Torah,* Abodah Zarah 1:1.

5. UNDER SENTENCE OF DEATH

1. The *Consolation* is itself written in alternating sections of prose and metrical verse (a form known as "prosimetrum").
2. That is, the qualities that distinguish a human being from animals on the one hand and God on the other.
3. These experiments, conducted by Michael Persinger, are briefly described and analyzed by P. S. Churchland in *Brain-Wise: Studies in Neurophilosophy* (Cambridge, Mass.: MIT Press, 2002), 381–89. See also A. Newberg, E. D'Acquili, and V. Rause, *Why God Won't Go Away: Brain Science and the Biology of Belief* (New York: Ballantine, 2001), 110–11.
4. Churchland, *Brain-Wise,* 385.
5. Richard S. Hallam, *Virtual Selves, Real Persons: A Dialogue Across Disciplines* (Cambridge: Cambridge University Press, 2009), 3. Similarly: "It is characteristic of our current regime of the self to reflect on and act on all the diverse domains, practices, and assemblages in terms of a unified 'personality,' an 'identity' to be revealed, discovered, or worked on in each. This machination of the self in terms of identity needs to be recognized as a regime of subjectification of recent origin," Nikolas Rose, *Inventing Our Selves: Psychology, Power, and Personhood* (Cambridge: Cambridge University Press, 1996), 39.
6. The contemporary philosopher Thomas Nagel has discussed one aspect of this question in a famous essay, "What Is It Like to Be a Bat?" *Philosophical Review* 83 (1974), 435–50, subsequently reprinted widely and easily found on the Internet.
7. David Marr, *Vision* (San Francisco: W. H. Freeman, 1982), cited in S. Pinker, *How the Mind Works* (New York: W. W. Norton, 1997), 213. See also D. Marr and H. K. Nishihara, "Representation and recognition of the spatial organization of three-dimension shapes," in *Proceedings of the Royal Society of London* (B 200), 269–94.
8. This act is (as current theorists endlessly warn) fraught with intellectual dangers, including what has been called "presentism," that is, studying other civilizations, past or present, "to produce a story which is the ratification, if not the glorification, of the [modern, Western] present": H. Butterfield, *The Whig Interpretation of History* (New York: W. W. Norton, 1963), v, cited in M. W. Conkey, "To Find Ourselves: Art and Social Geography in Prehistoric Hunter Gatherers," in C. Schrire, *Past and Present in Hunter Gatherer Studies* (New York: Academic Press, 1984), 258; cf. M. D. Sahlins, *'How Natives Think': Captain Cook, for Example* (Chicago: University

of Chicago Press, 1995); V. Li, *The Neo-Primitivist Turn: Critical Reflections on Alterity, Culture, and Modernity* (Toronto: University of Toronto Press, 2006). On the other hand, all we have in our attempt to understand a different sense of self—apart from introspection and the free play of our own imaginations—is the careful consideration of other societies and other times, that is, the evidence of ethnography and archaeology.

9. Scholars have sometimes questioned the validity of the very concept of hunter-gatherer societies. It certainly is true that "society" implies a degree of social organization often inappropriate to this phenomenon, and the use of the general category of "hunter-gatherer" obscured important differences separating different exemplars (e.g., in the matter of immediate vs. delayed gratification). For some of the ideological roots of this concept, see Alan Barnard, "Hunting-and-Gathering Society: an Eighteenth-Century Scottish Invention," in *idem, Hunter-Gatherers in History, Archaeology, and Anthropology* (New York: Berg, 2004), 31–43.

10. Rhys Jones, "The Tasmanian Paradox," in R. V. S. Wright, *Stone Tools as Cultural Markers: Change, Evolution, and Complexity* (Canberra: Australian Institute of Aboriginal Studies, 1977), 189–204. It should be noted that one of Jones's discoveries has been that even the Tasmanian aborigines, who used to be cited as a living example of the Stone Age, "Representatives of Palaeolithic Man" (to cite the title of a scientific paper delivered in 1893), actually underwent distinct changes and development in their way of life over the millennia—in part as a response to changes in climate and other physical conditions, and in part as a result of their own internal evolution: for example, they ceased to dwell in caves and built their own houses; they stopped eating fish. See Jones, "Hunters and History: A Case Study from Western Tasmania," in Schrire, *Past and Present in Hunter Gatherer Studies.*

11. Here the scholarly literature is too vast to mention; among many recent studies, see H. L. Cobb et al., *Investigating Prehistoric Hunter-Gatherer Identities* (BAR International Series 1411) (Oxford: Archaeopress, 2005); D. Papagianni et al., *Time and Change: Archaeological and Anthropological Perspectives on the Long-Term in Hunter-Gatherer Societies* (Oxford: Oxbow Books, 2008).

12. (I owe much of this description to M. Albert Abbadi.) An only slightly more complicated cosmology was observed among the Mbuti (or Bambuti) Pygmies of the Congo, whom the British anthropologist Colin Turnbull studied extensively: see his *The Forest People* (New York: Simon and Schuster, 1961), and *Wayward Servants* (Garden City, N. Y.: American Museum of Natural History, 1965). He reported that the Mbuti lack

any sacred hierarchy or magical rites such as are practiced by their Bantu neighbors (whom they regard as superstitious). The only numinous element in their lives is the patch of woodland in which they live. They "believe in a benevolent deity or supernatural power which they identify with the forest"; it is "regarded as the source of *pepo* [life force] and of their whole existence." When evil befalls them, it is because the forest is asleep; in such cases, the noisy *molimo* ritual is employed to wake the forest up.

6. "WHO SHALL I SAY IS CALLING?"

1. G. Lienhardt, *Divinity and Experience: The Religion of the Dinka* (Oxford: Oxford University Press, 1961), 28–31.
2. Ibid., 148.
3. Ibid., 149–50.
4. Daniel Dennett, "The Cartesian Theater and 'Filling In' the Stream of Consciousness," in Ned Block, Owen Flanagan, and Güven Güzeldere, *The Nature of Consciousness: Philosophical Debates* (Cambridge, Mass.: MIT Press, 1997), 83. In this connection, it might be worth mentioning here how various neurological disorders seem likewise to highlight the fragility of our own concept of the border between inside and outside. For example, patients suffering from *anosognosia* seem to lack any awareness that they have a neurological problem (most commonly hemiplegia, that is, paralysis or weakness of one side of the body following a stroke or other injury to the brain). Despite their paralysis, they insist that they can walk, move both arms, and in every way function as they did before the stroke. Clinicians similarly report on stroke patients who are unable to identify their paralyzed limbs as their own. "That's my brother's arm," they will say, or "my husband's arm" or it "belongs to the nurse" or "belongs to Mrs. D." In some cases, patients seeing the paralyzed limb as a foreign entity seek to expel it from their bed or request that it be surgically removed. See Todd E. Feinberg, *From Axons to Identity* (New York: W. W. Norton, 2009), 5–10; particularly interesting is his book's attempt to establish a connection between such a diffuse sense of where the "I" ends and the stages of child development, esp. 55–56.
5. This happened long before William Harvey's famous description of the circulatory system in 1628, through which it became clear that the basic role of the heart was to serve as the mere "pump" that made the circulatory system go.

6. Feinberg, *From Axons to Identity,* xi.
7. Daniel Dennett, "The Cartesian Theater," 84–93.

7. INTO THE STARK WORLD

1. Hence the New Testament's "Forgive us our debts as we forgive our debtors" (Matthew 6:12), versus the parallel "Forgive us our sins" in Luke 11:4. On this see Gary A. Anderson, *Sin: A History* (New Haven: Yale University Press, 2009), 27–39.
2. Here Augustine is arguing against Manichaean cosmology, which he espoused in his youth before his conversion to Christianity.
3. See on this C. Newsom, *The Self as Symbolic Space: Constructing Identity and Community at Qumran* (Leiden: Brill, 2004).

8. THE EERIE PROXIMITY

1. Note, however, that in narrating the same incident, the prophet Hosea calls Jacob's opponent an "angel"—or rather, in keeping with our theme, refers to the opponent as both God and an angel: "In his strength he fought with God, he struggled with an angel and overcame him" (Hosea 12:4–5).
2. Much later, at the end of the biblical period, does a very different sort of angel acquire names: Gabriel, Michael, Raphael, and so forth.
3. E. E. Evans-Pritchard, *Witchcraft, Oracles, and Magic Among the Azande,* abridged with an introduction by Eva Gillies (Oxford: Clarendon Press, 1976), 1–2, 18–19.
4. See Evans-Pritchard's discussion of this distinction in the next chapter.

9. THE SICKENING QUESTION

1. In Zoroastrianism, the good deity Ahura Mazda's opposite number is the wicked Angra Mainyu; see M. Boyce, *A History of Zoroastrianism: The Early Period* (Leiden: E. J. Brill, 1989).
2. H. Frankfort, *Before Philosophy: The Intellectual Adventure of Ancient Man* (New York: Penguin Books), 6–7.
3. Martha T. Roth, *Law Collections from Mesopotamia and Asia Minor* (Atlanta: Scholars Press, 1997). This prologue is clearly formulaic, mir-

rored in the far earlier Laws of Ur-Namma (A I 31–42); Laws of Lipit Ishtar; (I 1–37) Laws of Eshnunna (A 1–7); for all of these see Roth, *Law Collections,* 15, 24, 59, as well as the fragmentary neo-Assyrian texts published by A. K. Grayson and W. G. Lambert, "Akkadian Prophecies," *JCS* 18 (1964), "Anu [commanded] Enlil to establish justice. Justice will be established" (Text B, line 7).

4. The matter is never settled decisively in the Bible (see also Jeremiah 23:14; Sirach 16:8; 3 Maccabees 2:5; Wisdom 19:14; 2 Peter 2:6–7; Jude 7); also my *Traditions of the Bible,* 331–34.

5. Here I should note parenthetically that this absence of further information was felt to be a problem by the Bible's most ancient interpreters. Consequently, an interpretive tradition arose that the great evil done by the human beings had actually been spelled out in the previous paragraph, Genesis 6:1–4, which describes the mating of human females with the divine creatures called the "sons of God." But, as some modern scholars have justly pointed out, this paragraph is really the end of the long genealogical passage that precedes it and is quite unrelated to the Flood story. Its purpose is to explain where the amazing heroes of the past, the "men of renown" (*anshei shem*), came from: they had no known ancestry from the line of Enoch and Methuselah and so forth, but they must have come from somewhere. The Bible therefore recounts their hybrid, divine-human origins—which also explain how these "men of renown" were able to accomplish their extraordinary deeds. But none of this has any relation to the Flood story, which begins with the paragraph I cited: God simply saw human wickedness and decided to get rid of it, along with its perpetrators and, indeed, all of animal life.

6. Sometimes this answer was combined with others, as it was with the Azande. Thus, adversity may indeed often be explained as the result of witchcraft, but not *all* adversity; for example, violation of a taboo can bring about divine punishment—bringing us back to the connection of human sinfulness with evil. See Evans-Pritchard, *Witchcraft,* 27–29. The important point, however, is that even in such instances, adversity itself is not generated by the beneficent *Mbori,* the Supreme Being.

7. Including, for that matter, the atheist's answer: there is no God; life is altogether random and unjust. (Such a thought may appear altogether modern to some, but it has actually been around since antiquity. For example, it was put in the mouth of the murderous Cain in an ancient Bible translation as "There is no law and no Judge.")

10. AN END TO OMENS

1. This same phenomenon was noticed in a study of Polynesian religion by the anthropologist Alfred Gell (1945–97). Before Christianity came to Polynesia, he relates, "the immanence of the gods [i.e., the fact that they were conceived to dwell in this world] was the source of continuous anxiety . . . , and the rapidity and enthusiasm with which the Polynesians accomplished their conversion to Christianity stemmed from their untold relief upon discovering that God was, after all, transcendent, not part of this world . . . Polynesian ritual operated in precisely the inverse sense to Christian communion, i.e., the intention was to cause the divinity to leave (some part of) the world, rather than to induce the divinity to enter (some part of) it." A. Gell, "Closure and Multiplication: An Essay on Polynesian Cosmology and Ritual," in D. de Copper and Andre Iteanu, *Cosmos and Society in Oceania* (Oxford: Berg Publishing, 1995), 21–56.

2. On this inscription there is a surprisingly extensive literature, inter alia: F. M. Cross and R. J. Saley, "Phoenician Incantations on a Plaque of the Seventh Century B.C. from Arslan Tash in Upper Syria," *BASOR* 197 (1970), 42–49; D. Sperling, "An Arslan Tash Incantation: Interpretations and Implications," *HUCA* 53 (1982), 1–10; P. Amiet, "Observations sur les 'Tablettes magiques' d'Arslan Tash," *Aula Orientalis* 1 (1983), 109; B. W. Conklin, "Arslan Tash I and Other Vestiges of a Particular Syrian Incantatory Thread," *Biblica* 84 (2003).

3. See: J. Naveh and S. Shaked, *Amulets and Magical Bowls: Aramaic Inscriptions of Late Antiquity* (Jerusalem: Magnes, 1985); more generally, the recent dissertation of H. Frey-Anthes, *Unheilsmächte und Schutzgenien, Antiwesen und Grenzgänger: Vorstellungen von 'Dämonern' im alten Israel* (Freiburg: Academic Press, 2007).

4. All examples from Christophe Faraone, "The Agonistic Context of Early Greek Binding Spells," in C. Faraone and D. Obbinck, *Magika Hiera: Ancient Greek Magic and Religion* (New York: Oxford University Press, 1991), 13–14.

5. Evans-Pritchard, *Witchcraft, Oracles, and Magic,* 30–32.

6. This is the subject of a recent study from which some of the following examples are taken: Robert Bartlett, *The Natural and Supernatural in the Middle Ages* (Cambridge: Cambridge University Press, 2008). See also Peter Brown, "Society and the Supernatural: A Medieval Change," *Daedelus* 104 (1975), 133–51.

7. Midrash Tanhuma, *Naso,* 6.

8. *Entzauberung der Welt:* see Bartlett, 32–33. Even then, however, the movement was not unidirectional. While Aristotle's treatises on logic were uncontroversial, his writings on physics, biology, and other *libri naturales* were regarded with some suspicion and even, briefly, banned.

9. Caroline Bynum, *Metamorphosis and Identity* (New York: Zone Books, 2005), 91. She cites, among others, Benedicta Ward, *Miracles and the Medieval Mind: Theory, Record, and Event, 1000–1215* (Aldershot: Scolar, 1982), 4–10.

10. Bartlett, *Natural and Supernatural,* 52–59.

11. Ibid., 63.

12. A. Le Braz, *La Légende de la mort chez les bretons armoricains* (Paris: Belfond, 1966), 24–27.

13. C. Geertz, *The Interpretation of Cultures* (New York: Basic Books, 1973), 101.

14. Philippe Ariès, *Western Attitudes Toward Death* (Baltimore: Johns Hopkins University Press, 1974); *idem, The Hour of Our Death* (New York: Alfred A. Knopf, 1981). It may be useful to my overall subject if I cite here Ariès's own summary of his findings: "My hypothesis, which had already been proposed by Edgar Morin, was that there was *a relationship between man's attitude toward death and his awareness of self, of his degree of existence, or simply of his individuality.* This is the thread that has guided me through a dense and confusing mass of documents; this is the idea that has determined the itinerary that I followed to the end" (*Hour of Our Death,* 602; italics mine).

15. Ariès, *Hour of Our Death,* 98. As he suggests, the Jewish background of this text is obvious, and numerous parallels exist in later Jewish liturgy; the Christian references to Peter, Paul, and Thecla have been added at the end of this catalogue. (Thecla was an early Christian saint whose life was narrated in the apocryphal *Acts of Paul and Thecla.* The text recounts that Thecla, heeding Paul's advice, chose a life of chastity for herself, narrowly escaping death thanks to divine intervention.) See F. Bovon et al., *Les Actes apocryphes des apôtres: christianisme et le monde païen* (Geneva: Publications of the Theology Faculty of the University of Geneva no. 4; Labor et Fides, 1981).

16. Ariès, *Western Attitudes Toward Death,* 44–45.

17. "When we compare the present life of man on earth to that time of which we have no knowledge, it seems to me like the swift flight of a single sparrow through the banqueting hall where you are sitting at dinner on a winter's day with your thanes and counsellors. In the midst there is a

comforting fire to warm the hall; outside, the storms of winter rain or snow are raging. This sparrow flies swiftly in through one door of the hall, and out through another. While he is inside, he is safe from the winter storms; but after a few moments of comfort, he vanishes from sight into the wintry world from which he came. Even so, man appears on earth for a little while; but of what went before this life or of what follows, we know nothing." Bede, *Ecclesiastical History of the English People,* book 2, 13.

18. Ariès, *Hour of Our Death,* 116.

19. Sylvie-Anne Goldberg presents some surviving attestations of the *danse macabre* in Jewish sources: *Les deux rives du Yabbok: la maladie et la mort dans le judaïsme ashkénaze* (Paris: Editions du Cerf, 1989), 182–85.

20. Ariès, *Hour of Our Death,* 322.

21. Inter alia: Th. Jacobsen, *The Treasures of Darkness* (New Haven: Yale University Press, 1976), 147–64; A. R. Johnson, *The Vitality of the Individual in the Thought of Ancient Israel* (Eugene, Ore.: Wipf and Stock, 2006); Chester Starr, *Individual and Community: The Rise of the Polis, 800–500* (New York: Oxford University Press, 1986); Joseph Yacoub, "The Dignity of Individuals and of Peoples: The Contribution of Mesopotamia and of Syriac Heritage," *Diogenes* 215 (2007), 19–37; Colin Morris, *The Discovery of the Individual, 1050–1200* (London: SPCK, 1972); C. Bynum, "Did the Twelfth Century Discover the Individual?" *Journal of Ecclesiastical History* 31 (1980), 1–17; Georges Duby and Ph. Braunstein, "The Emergence of the Individual," in Duby, *Representations of the Medieval World,* vol. 2 (Cambridge, Mass.: Harvard University Press, 1988); J. G. Weiger, *The Individuated Self: Cervantes and the Emergence of the Individual* (Columbus: Ohio University Press, 1979); A. Renaut, *The Era of the Individual: A Contribution to a History of Subjectivity* (Princeton, N.J.: Princeton University Press, 1997); N. Z. Davis, "Boundaries and Sense of Self in Sixteenth-Century France," in Thomas C. Heller et al., *Reconstructing Individualism: Autonomy, Individuality, and the Self in Western Thought* (Stanford, Calif.: Stanford University Press, 1986), 53–63; A. Banani and S. Vryonis, *Individualism and Conformity in Classical Islam* (Wiesbaden: Otto Harrassowitz, 1977).

22. Ariès, *Hour of Our Death,* 559–601. While Ariès associates the denial of death with mainline British society, he seeks to identify in America two somewhat contrary tendencies at work, whereby the "complete erasure of death" from daily life competes with the resurfacing of a transmogrified version of the old Romantic theme of "your own death."

11. MEDICAL MAGIC

1. M. Mauss, *A General Theory of Magic* (New York: Routledge, 2001), 36.
2. Inter alia: Anne Harrington, *The Placebo Effect: An Interdisciplinary Approach* (Cambridge, Mass.: Harvard University Press, 1997).
3. Richard Seltzer, *Mortal Lessons: Notes on the Art of Surgery* (New York: Touchstone, 1974), 33–36.
4. This last is associated with the classical study of W. Robertson Smith, *Lectures on the Religion of the Semites* (London: A. & C. Black, 1894). See in general: E. E. Evans-Pritchard, *Nuer Religion* (New York: Oxford University Press, 1956), 272–90; S. Atran, *In Gods We Trust* (New York: Oxford University Press, 2002), 114–19.
5. See J. Levenson, *The Death and Resurrection of the Beloved Son* (New Haven: Yale University Press, 1993).
6. See my *In Potiphar's House* (Cambridge, Mass.: Harvard University Press, 1990), 185.
7. Walter Burkert, *Creation of the Sacred: Tracks of Biology in Early Religions* (Cambridge, Mass.: Harvard University Press, 1996), 37.
8. Ibid., 38.

Index

Page numbers beginning with 209 refer to endnotes.

Index

Aramaic language, 27n, 162
Arcadia, 197
archeology, 22, 33–34, 68, 69, 111–14,
 163, 215
architecture, medieval, 95–96, 114,
 131
Ariès, Philippe, 175, 177–78, 180–81,
 183, 220–21
Aristotle, 167, 220
Arslan Tash, 162
art:
 cave, 22
 medieval, 95–96, 131, 178
 post-Renaissance, 55
 prehistoric, 22, 70
 religious, 95–96, 116, 178
 Renaissance, 96, 99
"Art of Dying, The," 178
Ashtoret, 157
Assyrians, 129, 137
astrology, 170, 172
astronomy, 104
atheism, 44, 218
Auden, W. H., 32
Augustine, Saint, 97–99, 181, 217
Australian Aborigines, 69–70
autonomic nervous system, 78
Azande, 124–26, 164–65, 169, 218

Baal, 28, 133, 157
Babylon, 136, 196
Babylonians, 129, 134–35, 169, 196,
 204
"background music": 2, 4, 9–11, 12,
 13, 20, 27, 43, 74, 131, 182
baptism, 97
Bedouins, 111
behavior patterns, innate, 52, 84, 85,
 211
Berechiah, R. 108

Berger, Peter, 30–31, 209–10
Bezalel, Yehudah Loew b. Maharal
 of Prague, 80
Bible, 14, 29, 74, 92–94, 107, 141–52
 ancient interpretive traditions of,
 97, 218
 King James version of, 15–16,
 39n, 74
 miracles in, 168
 reading and interpretation of,
 96–99, 111, 126–29, 157, 168
 Vetus Latina version of, 97–99
 Vulgate version of, 97, 109
 see also Hebrew Bible; New
 Testament; Pentateuch; specific
 biblical books
birds, killing of, 156–57, 192, 194
Blackfoot Indians, 197
body:
 burial of, 21–22, 30, 33, 70, 71, 176
 cremation of, 22n, 181
 fitting within the borders of, 27,
 43, 203
 healing of, 21, 193–94
 organs and parts of, 47, 61, 62, 77,
 78, 79
 resurrection of, 177n, 209
 soul and, 61–62
Boethius, Anicius Manlius Severinus,
 56–59, 82–84, 203
 trial and execution of, 56–57, 59,
 140
Book of Jubilees, 160–61, 170
Bororo Indians, 31–32
Boston, Mass., 2, 185–86
Bradley, Mr., 60n–61n
brain, 34, 45
 bicameral structure of, 65–66, 79
 Broca's area of, 65
 cellular material of, 80, 81

Index

Index

Index

Index

smiling, universality of, 50
societies:
  non-Western, 68–71
  organization of, 66, 68, 69–71
  primitive, 68–71, 215–16
  Western, 68, 86
Sodom, 127, 149–51
sodomy, 150
Solomon, King, 14
sorcery, 56, 169
soul, 21, 26, 61–63, 85, 90, 94, 97,
    101–2, 115
  body and, 61–62
  healing of, 21
  judgment of, 178
  "modern," 72, 86
  open vs. closed, 86
  origins of, 72
  pineal gland as seat of, 79
  returning to God of, 62–63,
    176–77
  semipermeable, 72, 78, 81, 193
spandrel, 46–47
speech, 21, 47–49, 68, 84, 106
  see also language
spirits, 33, 65, 71, 75
  ancestral, 35, 66
  evil, 161–63
spirituality, 90, 99
spiritual possession, 60, 76
Starry Night (van Gogh), 99
Stoic philosophy, 83–84
Sudan (and the Dinka), 74–77
Sullivan, Arthur, 5
sun, 46, 74, 87, 99, 104, 108, 158, 160,
    182, 204
  eclipse of, 169, 170
supernatural world, 161–75, 187
  breaking the spell of, 167–71
  natural law vs., 164–65, 166

  see also angels; curses; evil; occult
    forces; witchcraft
superstition, 140, 165–75, 216
surgery, 188, 189
Syria, 162
Syro-African rift, 150

Tai Chi, 193
Talmud, 186
tape measures, spring-loaded, 12, 13,
    140
Tasmanian Aborigines, 69–70, 215
technology, 68, 69, 155, 182
tectonic plates, 150
Teiresias, 202
temples, 4–5, 21, 23, 65, 166–67, 194,
    204
  musicians of, 196
  presence of God in, 4–5
  priests of, 65, 166
Ten Commandments, 157
Ten Plagues, 168
Testament of Levi, 108
Testaments of the Twelve Patriarchs,
    The, 175–76
Thecla, Saint, 177, 220
Theodoric, Emperor of Rome, 56
Thietmar, Bishop of Merseburg,
    170
toadstools, 173–74
"To an Athlete Dying Young"
    (Housman), 7–9
tombs, 163
tools, 68, 69, 155
touch, 78
Tower of Babel, 127
Tractatus Logico-Philosophicus
    (Wittgenstein), 105–6
trials by ordeal, 166–67, 168
Trinity, 160

236

Index

About the Author

James L. Kugel is Starr Professor of Hebrew Literature at Harvard University, emeritus. He is the author of a number of books of biblical scholarship, including *How to Read the Bible* (2007), *The God of Old* (2003), *The Great Poems of the Bible* (1999), and *The Bible as It Was* (1997). In 2001, Kugel was awarded the prestigious Grawemeyer Prize in Religion. He lives in Jerusalem, Israel.